teach®

home education

home education
deborah durbin

Launched in 1938, the **teach yourself** series grew rapidly in response to the world's wartime needs. Loved and trusted by over 50 million readers, the series has continued to respond to society's changing interests and passions and now, 70 years on, includes over 500 titles, from Arabic and Beekeeping to Yoga and Zulu. What would you like to learn?

be where you want to be with **teach yourself**

For UK order enquiries: please contact Bookpoint Ltd, 130 Milton Park, Abingdon, Oxon OX14 4SB. Telephone: +44 (0) 1235 827720. Fax: +44 (0) 1235 400454. Lines are open 09.00–17.00, Monday to Saturday, with a 24-hour message answering service. Details about our titles and how to order are available at www.teachyourself.co.uk

Long renowned as the authoritative source for self-guided learning – with more than 50 million copies sold worldwide – the **teach yourself** series includes over 500 titles in the fields of languages, crafts, hobbies, business, computing and education.

British Library Cataloguing in Publication Data: a catalogue record for this title is available from the British Library.

First published in UK 2009 by Hodder Education, part of Hachette UK, 338 Euston Road, London, NW1 3BH.

This edition published 2009.

The **teach yourself** name is a registered trade mark of Hodder Headline.

Typeset by Transet Limited, Coventry, England.
Printed in Great Britain for Hodder Education, an Hachette UK Company, 338 Euston Road, London NW1 3BH, by CPI Cox & Wyman, Reading, Berkshire RG1 8EX.

The publisher has used its best endeavours to ensure that the URLs for external websites referred to in this book are correct and active at the time of going to press. However, the publisher and the author have no responsibility for the websites and can make no guarantee that a site will remain live or that the content will remain relevant, decent or appropriate.

Hachette UK's policy is to use papers that are natural, renewable and recyclable products and made from wood grown in sustainable forests. The logging and manufacturing processes are expected to conform to the environmental regulations of the country of origin.

Impression number   10 9 8 7 6 5 4 3 2 1
Year   2012 2011 2010 2009

contents

v

dedication

To my three wonderful daughters Rebecca, Georgina and Holly. Without whom I would never have experienced the wonderful world that is home education.

acknowledgements

When I first started out in home education I was clueless as to what it entailed; so it is with thanks to all the educational charities for their information and support that I now feel qualified to write this book. I would also like to thank my daughter, Rebecca, for initially bringing the idea to my attention that an education can be more than just school, and to my three daughters for making this experience such a fun and inspiring one.

My thanks go out to Iris Harrison who fought (and continues to fight) tooth and nail for the rights of parents to educate their children from home; to Dr. Paula Rothermel for her research and study into home education; to all the other professionals for their insight and research into the subject; and to all the wonderful charities, groups and organizations dedicated to home educating. I would also like to thank my mum, Barbara, for her insight into learning styles; my sister, Helen, for her infectious enthusiasm; Harry Scoble, Lisa Grey, Katie Roden and all at Hodder for allowing me to just get on with it; and of course to my husband, Richard, for his continued patience and for cooking sausage casserole for me when I've been too busy to eat!

introduction

> *Education is not the filling of a pail, but the lighting of a fire.*
>
> William Butler Yeats

Driving home from a day out at the zoo, my youngest daughter looked out of the car window and said, 'Look at those poor children Mummy, they're all locked up in a cage. That must be awful.' She was in fact referring to a school we had just driven past which had a huge wire fence around it. Of course, my daughter has never experienced an education within the confines of a school fence. In her young eyes, the children playing in the playground were locked up in a cage, much like the lions that we had just seen at the zoo.

When you sit and look at the world through a child's eyes, you begin to see things in a different way and may even begin to question the 'norm'. Although I explained that the fence was merely a precaution to ensure that the children were safe whilst they were in school, my daughter only saw it as a restriction, to stop the children from getting out and being free. To a child who has never experienced school it looked as though the children were locked up and all being forced to do the same thing.

In the four years that I have educated our three children at home, I can honestly say that we have all had a ball. Their unconventional learning has led them to learn about things that they would never have had the advantage to learn otherwise. I call them my free-range children, because that is what they are: they are free to learn and explore the world naturally without the confines or restrictions of a wire fence.

Although this is my own experience of educating our children at home, it has not always been like this…

Case study: Worcester Crown Court Appeal 1981

'We arrived at the Court to a circus of television cameras and journalists and then entered the silence of the Court foyer. Geoff immediately went into the men's toilets. Standing next to him was a very tall, heavily-built, impressive man dressed in a long black gown with a massive volume of black hair on his head and a huge black beard. Without introducing himself he said to Geoff as they stood there, 'I am absolutely with you. My son has the same problem as your children (dyslexia) and I wish you all the luck in the world.' They walked from the toilets together and to a group of journalists, he said, 'Have sympathy with this case. My son is also like these children.' This man was the Clerk of the Court and his first job after we entered Court number one was to ask "Are you the Appellant Geoffrey George Harrison and the Appellant Iris Harrison?" We both replied in the affirmative and so the case began…'

The above is a true account of the court case that took place at Worcester Crown Court because Iris and Geoff Harrison wanted the best education for their children and wouldn't back down to the threats of having their children taken into care from their Local Authority.

Many people do not realize that home education is legal in most countries. Most assume that they *have* to send their children to school regardless of the fact that a standard and basic education might not be suitable to their educational needs.

Home educating has always been legal in the UK and the right to home educate your child has been reaffirmed in recent Acts of Parliament. In 1996 the Education Act was updated to replace the 1944 Act owing to an appeal case between Iris Harrison and Geoff Harrison versus Stevenson.

It is thanks to Iris Harrison and her husband that parents are able to educate their children from home without being hauled before the courts and threatened with having their children taken away. They are widely considered to be the pioneers in home education. Iris was one of the founders of Education Otherwise – the biggest home education charity in the UK.

Iris and Geoff withdrew their daughter from school because she could not cope with the level of literacy that she was expected to learn. Iris said that her daughter had changed from a loving and gentle child into a monster in only a matter of days of being at the school. She later discovered that her daughter was profoundly dyslexic and because the school was not familiar with symptoms of dyslexia they didn't know that her daughter could learn better 'doing', rather than being told what to do.

The Harrison's Local Education Authority didn't agree and told them that they must send their child to school or face the consequences. The consequences being that they would take all of the four children into care, including the youngest who was still a baby.

It sounds like something out of a movie – faced with the prospect of having their children taken away or sending their daughter to school, Iris and her husband resorted to running away with the children to a remote island in Scotland. There they lived in a small hut with no running water. Their daughter learned how to read by reading old copies of the Exchange & Mart.

Deciding that a hut stuck in the middle of nowhere with no running water and was not the answer, Iris and Geoff moved back to England in the hope that all the fuss had died down. It hadn't. The Local Education Authority again threatened to take all their children into care. Iris said that the local authority (LA) was like the Gestapo and recalls that she even resorted to buying a flock of geese just to keep the inspectors away from the house. Iris felt that an institutionalized education did nothing but harm her children and refused to give in to the LA.

The LA had no grounds on which to suspect that Iris and Geoff were nothing but caring and loving parents, but because they would not back down and send their children to school, they continued to harass them. After several more months, Iris demanded that they take her to court and let the court decide whether or not they could educate their children in a way that they, as parents, felt appropriate. Iris knew that an independent case would be a safer bet than believing the LA. They instructed a lawyer to represent them in court.

The 1944 Education Act provided the loophole that the Harrisons needed – the Act stated that every school-aged child should receive a full-time education suitable to his age and ability, 'either by regular attendance at school or otherwise'. It was this one sentence that enabled the Harrison's to continue to educate their children from home.

The judge at the case defined a 'suitable education' as one which was such as to:

1 Prepare the children for life in modern civilized society, and
2 Enable them to achieve their full potential.

Section 7 of the Education Act 1996, which applies to England and Wales, now states that:

'The parent of every child of compulsory school age shall cause him to receive efficient full-time education suitable to:

His age, ability and aptitude, and

Any special educational needs he may have, either by regular attendance at school or otherwise.'

In layman terms this means that parents are not obliged to send their child to school to be educated and can legally provide their child with an education at home. The law is the same for Northern Ireland. Scottish law states that 'every child has the right to an education, and it is the duty of the parent of every school aged child to provide an education, either by sending the child to school, or by other means.'

Today, Iris's children are in their 30s: one trained in alternative medicine, another runs an ironworks workshop, one now renovates classic cars and another teaches new skills to young people.

Of the court case, Iris has said that it was the worst time of her life, but is thankful that by going to court against the LA other parents will not have to go through the same hell that she did just because they don't believe that an institutionalized education is the right one for their children.

Regardless of what some may tell you, or what you may read in the press, no one is sure of the exact figure of home-educated children in the UK. The charity Education Otherwise claim that it is 50,000, other educational academics claim that it could be much higher. Exact figures are not known due to the fact that many children have never been registered at a school so have therefore never been counted. There are also many children from travelling families that have never received a formal education As more parents are realizing that there is a legal alternative to state-funded schools it is thought that this figure will rise significantly within the next few years.

Parents that choose to educate their children at home do not have to be trained teachers, nor do you need any special qualifications. You do not have to follow the National Curriculum that is set by the government for state-funded schools and you do not have to follow guidelines, do standard assessment tests (SATS), exams, keep to term times or adhere to school timetables.

You are not required to provide any particular type of education and you are under no obligation to have special premises, cover the same syllabus as schools, observe school hours, give formal lessons, seek permission to home educate, inform your Local Authority (unless your child has already been registered at a school), or have regular contact with the Local Authority.

There is no single reason as to why parents choose to home educate their children, some are dissatisfied with class sizes, others are concerned with the issue of testing children to meet governmental standards. Some parents disagree with their children only being able to learn at the level of the average student and others feel that their children require a more specialist education which the school cannot provide effectively. Others have issues with bullying and abuse in schools and for some their reasons to home educate are religious.

The majority of people that teach their children at home do so because they have been failed one way or another by the state-funded education system. They often do not have the financial resources to be able to afford private education, so home education is often the answer.

Top tip

The charity Education Otherwise (**www.education-otherwise. org**) has lots of free information available for parents thinking of home educating their children.

There are many advantages to educating a child in their own home. Studies have shown that home-educated children learn quicker, are more sociable and happier, and are more independent than those children who are educated by the State.

Teach Yourself Home Education is a guide for anyone who wants to home educate their child/children. This book will tell you everything you need to know about home schooling and includes some case studies from other parents who have chosen to educate their children from home.

It also includes your legal rights to home educate, practical advice as to the many different teaching and learning styles that home educators use, frequently asked questions and the pros and cons of being a home educator.

Top tip

Remember: Your child must be educated, but school is not compulsory.

Case study: My own story

When I was growing up there was never a mention of home education. It was accepted by everyone, and still often is, that children start school at the age of five and stay there until they are 16. The lucky few with wealthy parents went to boarding school or were educated at private schools with low class numbers. The only time I remember hearing about someone being educated at home was when we studied the life and times of Beatrix Potter in English Literature and discovered that she was home educated. Other than that, the only time I had ever heard about being home educated or tutored was on a children's television programme about a child growing up in a travelling circus.

Even when my own children were born in the 1990s, the subject of home schooling was never mentioned. We assumed, like most parents, I would imagine, that our children would go to the school nearest to where we lived and this is what they did.

Even as I write this, I still find it strange that as parents we are very careful about the selection process when sending our children to nursery or pre-school – meeting the staff, making sure that our children are going to be happy there – and yet when they turn five most of us automatically put them into the nearest school without a second thought as to whether that particular school is going to be in their best interest.

I'll be honest, I've never been a fan of state-funded schools and have always thought that the system was badly designed. How many other organizations do you know that expect an individual to sit in a small room with 30 other individuals and be made to learn a subject to the level of everyone else in that room, whether they want to or not? Having said this, I knew of no legal alternative for one-to-one learning.

It was our eldest daughter who originally brought the idea of being educated at home to us. She had always followed the rules and kept her head down, but she was never happy at school and couldn't wait for three o'clock to come round so that she could be out of there. She was due to start at the local comprehensive school in the September and had a disastrous induction day. So disastrous that she declared there and then that she was never going to go back there and presented us with the idea of learning at home.

Like most parents who knew nothing about the subject, our initial response was, 'You can't do that!'

'Yes, I can actually,' our daughter replied, 'Look!', and she presented us with numerous website addresses about home education to study. It was the school summer holidays and we spent much of the time reading pages and pages of information about the various aspects of home schooling. The more we read the more it made sense.

Why were we pushing her to learn subjects that she had little or no interest in just because the government had decided that this is what she must be taught? Why were we allowing the school to insist that she should 'play nicely' with a child who had spat in her face earlier that day? In every area in her home life we had taught her to question if she felt that something was unfair and yet if she dared to air her views in the classroom she would get told off for it.

The more we looked into home schooling the more determined and happier our daughter got at the prospect of never having to return to school.

Like every parent, I worried and questioned everything. How was I going to teach her what she needed to know? (I'm a trained journalist, not a trained teacher.) Would she miss out on the social aspects of school? Would I have to learn Russian, woodwork or circus skills? I had no one to ask because there was no one around that I knew who taught their children from home. However,

I did notice how much happier and less stressed my daughter was already becoming. I contacted a home educating charity that I had found on the Internet and voiced my concerns; in particular, knowing how fickle children can be, I wanted to know what to do if our daughter suddenly decided that she didn't like the idea of home schooling any more. 'Well, send her back to school,' was the reply. It all seemed so simple then.

September came and armed with as much information as I could find and a truckload of Key Stage 3 workbooks, a copy of the National Curriculum and enough stationary to supply *Staples*, I nervously penned a letter to the head teacher to say that my daughter would no longer require a place at the school.

That was four years ago. In that time our other two daughters have decided to follow suit – we de-registered our middle daughter six months after our eldest daughter left school and our youngest daughter has never experienced life inside the school gates.

Do we have any regrets? Only that we didn't know about home education before. The Key Stage 3 books have remained unopened because we have found that our children learn better studying what they want to study and when. Their days are filled with playing games of Monopoly (maths), ice skating (PE), trying not to blow up the house (science), visiting countries (geography), playing Sims (IT skills), attending concerts and going backstage (music), breeding tropical fish (biology/marine science), writing novels (English language), reading daily newspapers (media studies), watching world documentaries (culture and citizenship) and much more.

And so, this book is aimed to guide you through the steps to educating your child/children from home. It will explain what's involved and show you how you too can successfully home educate.

Top tip

Give yourself and your child time to get used to the idea of being home educated. Don't do as I did and buy loads of learning materials that may well not get used. Instead, see how you get on and buy learning adjuncts as you need them.

In case you're interested, here are some famous people that have been home educated:

Beatrix Potter (author), Patrick Moore (astronomer), Daniel and Natasha Bedingfield (singers), Noël Coward (actor), Agatha Christie (author), Charles Dickens (author), Whoopi Goldberg (actor), Jennifer Love Hewitt (actor), Mozart (composer), Louis Armstrong (musician), Claude Monet (artist), Leonardo da Vinci (artist), Florence Nightingale (nurse), Charles Chaplin (actor).

Key points

- The number of home-educated children in the UK is estimated to be around 50,000.
- Educating your child from home is legal in England and Wales.
- As a parent you are obliged by law to provide your child with an education suitable to his/her age and ability. This does not necessarily mean that he/she has to go to school for that education.

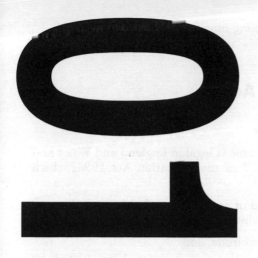

01

the legalities

In this chapter you will learn:
- about the Education Act
- about countries where home education is illegal
- about employment laws relating to children.

I have never let schooling interfere with my education.

Mark Twain

The Education Act

England and Wales

Educating your child at home is legal in England and Wales and is covered under Section 7 of the Education Act 1996, which states:

'The parent of every child of compulsory school age shall cause him to receive efficient full-time education suitable to:

(a) His age, ability and aptitude, and
(b) Any special educational needs he may have, either by regular attendance at school or otherwise.'

You can see the full Act by looking up the Education Act via the Office of Public Sector Information website (**www.opsi.gov.uk**) but essentially it says:

- If you have a school-aged child, you must ensure that he/she is educated.
- The child's education provided must be efficient and full-time.
- You can delegate this duty to a school, or you can do it yourself.
- The education must be suitable to your child's age and abilities.
- If your child has special educational needs, you must cater for these.

Nowhere within the Act does it specify what an education is, so just because the state-funded schools follow the National Curriculum, which is theoretically a standard set of learning rules set by the education department, the Act does not say that you are obliged to adopt that way of learning.

A suitable education was clarified in the appeal case between Iris Harrison and Geoff Harrison versus Stevenson which was heard at Worcester Crown Court in 1981 when the parents who were convicted of not sending their child to school appealed against their convictions for failure to comply with school attendance orders. The judge declared that an education must be suitable to a child's age, ability and aptitude and must:

1 Prepare the child for life in a modern civilized society, and
2 Enable them to achieve their full potential.

Although the Act is rather generalized, this case set the precedent for parents who were unhappy with the way their children were being educated and now allows them to educate them in a way that they feel will benefit them more. Due to the vagueness of the Act, some critics would say that it does leave a child at risk if parents fail to send their children to school and fail to provide them with any education at home. However, these cases are very rare and the majority of parents who choose to educate their children from home do so because their children have been let down by the state-funded system in some way.

Just as every child is an individual, so too are the reasons why they or their parents have chosen home education and we will look more deeply into this in Chapter 02. Provided your child is not registered at a school you are not bound by any other constraints within the Act as to how you choose to educate your child. You are not required by law to have formal permission to educate your child from home, neither do you have to inform your Local Authority (LA) – we will discuss more about the LA later in the book. You are not required by law to have any prior teacher training, nor do you have to be qualified or cover the same syllabus as a school. The Act does not dictate how you should educate your child, that is up to you and your child. So if your child harbours dreams of being an artist and just wants to learn how to paint for a year, that is considered an education because it is enabling your child to fulfil their full potential in a subject of their choice.

Also within the Act it does not state that you have to keep to school hours, term times or a fixed timetable, so if your son or daughter prefers to learn during the evenings, or weekends, thus freeing up the days for day trips, that is also fine.

As long as your child is in full-time education and is learning to a standard to suit their age and ability you can teach and learn how, when and where you want. Even a trip to the supermarket and working out the correct amount of money for the groceries can be put under the subject heading of Maths.

Section 7 of the 1996 Act states that if you have a child already registered as a pupil at a school, you have a duty under section 444 to ensure that he/she attends that school regularly and during the school opening hours. This clause is to prevent the issue of truancy and if you fail to abide by this you are guilty of a criminal offence and could be taken to court. This section also applies to children who are educated at home, so you can't declare your child is home educated only to allow them to wander the street and not provide them with any form of education.

Every school is required by law (Education Regulations 1995 SI 1995/2089) to have a register of the pupils that attend that school and to keep admissions and attendance records. Any child who is named on that register is therefore a registered pupil, meaning that they are required by law to attend the regular hours of that particular school. If you decide that you no longer wish your child to attend that school, you are required by the Act to de-register your child. We will look at the process of de-registering your child in Chapter 05.

Top tip

As a parent you are obliged by law to provide your child with an education suitable to his/her age and ability. This does not necessarily mean that he/she has to go to school for that education.

Scotland

The legislation relating to education in Scotland is found in the Education (Scotland) Act 1980 and the 2000 Standards in Scotland's Schools etc. Act. The section outlines the legislation relevant to home education and appears to be more updated and positive than English educational laws.

Section 14 of the Standards in Scotland's Schools etc. Act states that:

'The Scottish Ministers may issue guidance as to the circumstances in which parents may choose to educate their children at home; and education authorities shall have regard to any such guidance.'

This guidance is issued under Section 14 of the Standards in Scotland's Schools etc. Act 2000. This means that education authorities must have regard to the guidance.

Section 1 and 2 of the Act states that:

1 It shall be the right of every child of school age to be provided with school education by, or by virtue of arrangements made, or entered into, by, an education authority.

2 (1) Where school education is provided to a child or young person by, or by virtue of arrangements made, or entered into, by, an education authority it shall be the duty of the authority to secure that the education is directed to the development of the personality, talents and mental and physical abilities of the child or young person to their fullest potential.

(2) In carrying out their duty under this section, an education authority shall have due regard, so far as is reasonably practicable, to the views (if there is a wish to express them) of the child or young person in decisions that significantly affect that child or young person, taking account of the child or young person's age and maturity.

Section 30 of the Education (Scotland) Act 1980 stipulates that:

1 It shall be the duty of the parent of every child of school age to provide efficient education for him suitable to his age, ability and aptitude either by causing him to attend a public school regularly or by **other means**.

2 Section 1 of the Standards in Scotland's Schools etc. Act 2000 (right of child to be provided with school education by, or by virtue of arrangements made by, an education authority) is without prejudice to the choice afforded a parent by subsection (1) above.

As with English law, parents are responsible for providing their children with an education. Whether they choose to do that by passing that duty on to a mainstream school or privately is up to them.

Scottish law is similar to English law in that if your child has not attended a state school in the area you are not obliged to get consent from them and you do not need permission from anyone if:

- your child has never attended a state-funded school
- your child has never attended a state-funded school in that authority's area

- your child is being withdrawn from an independent school
- your child has finished primary education in one school but has not started secondary education in another
- he school your child has been attending has closed.

In Scottish law, if you are withdrawing your child from a state school, they will recommend the granting or refusal of 'consent' based on the education provision you have outlined.

Northern Ireland

The law in Northern Ireland is much the same as in England and Wales and the legislation almost identical, although there is nothing in Northern Ireland law that states that a parent must secure permission for de-registering their child. The law relating to home education for Northern Ireland is set out in the Education and Libraries Northern Ireland Order 1986 SI 1968/594, Section 45, which states:

'The parent of every child of compulsory school age shall cause him to receive efficient full-time education suitable to his age, ability and aptitude and to any special educational needs he may have, either by regular attendance at school or otherwise.'

Schedule 13 – Enforcement of duty imposed by article 45, states:

1 Where it appears to a board that a parent of a child of compulsory school age in its area is failing to perform the duty imposed on him by article 45(1), the board shall serve on the parent a notice requiring him, within such period not being less than 14 days from the service of the notice, to satisfy the board that the child is, by regular attendance or otherwise, receiving efficient full-time education suitable to his age, ability and aptitude and to any special educational needs he may have, either by regular attendance at school or otherwise.

2 Where, at any time whilst a school attendance order is in force with respect to a child, the parent of the child makes an application to the board by whom the order was made requesting ... that the order be revoked on the ground that arrangements have been made for the child to receive otherwise than at school education suitable to his age, ability and aptitude and to any special educational needs he may have, the board shall amend or revoke the order in compliance with the request unless it is of the opinion that:

– no satisfactory arrangements have been made for the education of the child otherwise than at school.

> **Top tip**
>
> Home education is a legal alternative in the UK. Don't let other people tell you otherwise.

Countries where home education is illegal

Home schooling is legal in most countries but recently the state of California in the United States has made it illegal on the grounds that parents are not certified teachers.

Educating your child from home is also illegal in Germany, Brazil and in Hong Kong (for Hong Kong citizens). Many parents get round this law by opening their own private schools.

> **Top tip**
>
> There are many home-educating resources on the Internet including groups and charities that will provide you with the information you need. Type 'home education' into any search engine and you will find a whole host of results.

Children and employment

Just like school-educated children, some home-educated children wish to earn a bit of pocket money during their free time and the legislation relating to employment and children is complex, but the government have issued the following information for children that wish to work. This is designed to protect the employment rights of children and young people. The laws relating to the employment of children are very strict and an employer can be prosecuted for breaking them. The laws for all children, whether educated at school or at home, are the same.

The age at which children can leave full-time education is about to change from 16 to 17 by 2013 and 18 by 2015. No one under the minimum school leaving age can be employed in work other than light work. Children are not allowed to do any work that can be viewed as harmful to their safety, health or development. Children are not allowed to:

- work in a factory
- do any work involving transport
- work in a mine
- work on a merchant ship
- work in any area that is designed for adult customers, for example, a pub, a betting shop or a casino
- go door-to-door canvassing or work within an amusement arcade.

Term time

Children are not allowed to work during school/education hours. They are not allowed to work between the time of 7 a.m. and 7 p.m. or for more than one hour before traditional school hours. Children cannot work for more than four hours without taking a break of at least one hour.

During standard term time children are allowed to work a maximum of 12 hours per week. They are only allowed to work a maximum of two hours on school days and on Sundays and a maximum of five hours on Saturdays for 13–14 year olds, or eight hours for 15–16 year olds.

Summer holidays

During the summer holidays 13–14 year olds are allowed to work a maximum of 25 hours per week of which up to a maximum of five hours per day for weekdays and Saturdays and a maximum of two hours on a Sunday. However, 15–16 year olds are allowed to work up to 35 hours per week.

Children are not allowed to work without having a two-week break from any work during the summer holidays in any one calendar year.

Wages

The national minimum wage is currently (2009) £4.60 an hour for 18–21 year olds and £5.52 an hour for 22 year olds and over. Children aged 16–17 receive £3.40 per hour but there is no minimum wage set for children under the age of 16.

Legal requirements

Employers are required by law to inform the education department of the Local Authority (LA) that they are employing a school-aged child. If the LA is happy with the arrangements they will issue the child an employment permit – a child is not insured without one. The permit must be signed by both the employer and one of the parents. Children do not need a work permit for work experience.

The Local Authority where you live may also have some extra rules called by-laws regarding the employment of children in your area and you should check with them with regards to employment laws for children. By-laws will state whether or not children are allowed to work in trading and will specify how many hours they can work, on which days and the places that they may work.

Children under 13

The youngest age your child can work part-time is 13 years old, with the exception of children involved in television, theatre, the modelling industry or similar activities. If a child is offered work in these areas, they will need to get a performance licence. Performance licences are issued by the LA. Before granting a licence the LA will liaise with the head teacher of the child's school to ensure that the child's education will not suffer should that licence be granted.

The future of home education

Unless the Education Act is amended again, home education will continue to be a legal alternative in the UK and charities such as Education Otherwise and the organization Freedom for Children to Grow – a campaign to protect a parent's choice to educate their children at home and against unnecessary changes in the law that would infringe their current freedoms – endeavour to fight the right of choice in education, despite the Department for Education and Skills stating publically that, 'We believe the best place to educate a child is actually in school.'

Updates of any news relating to home schooling can be found on the websites of various charities and organizations which are detailed in Chapter 11.

Top tip

Keep up to date with the laws relating to education by visiting the Department for Children, Schools and Families website at **www.dcsf.gov.uk**

Key points

- You can legally educate your child from home.
- No child is allowed to do paid work if they are under 13 years old.
- Home education is not legal in every county.

02

the benefits

Great spirits have always been violently oppressed by mediocre minds.

Albert Einstein

Who does it?

There are many varied reasons as to why a parent chooses to educate their child/children at home.

It is a misconception that *all* home-educated children have been bullied at school. It is also not true that *all* home-educated children are children with special needs or that all home-educating parents are a bit 'hippy dippy', or belong to a travelling circus!

Home-educating parents come in many guises and are just normal people doing normal, everyday jobs, just like any other parent of a child. Some are professionals, others are stay-at-home-mums/dads, some, like myself, work from home, others run their own businesses, some work night shifts so that they can teach their children during the day. The only difference between a home-educating parent and any other parent is that they are in charge of their children's education.

It is also a fallacy that home-educating parents must be well off. Many home-educating parents that I know have to juggle jobs in order to be at home during schooling hours. Many couples schedule their hours so that one parent is at home whilst the other works. This could mean one parent working days and the other working evenings/nights. There are very few families that can afford not to work but this does not necessarily mean that it has to prevent you from educating your child at home.

Funding

Regardless of how much a family earn, a state-funded school receives funding every year for every child that attends that school. Parents who educate their children from home receive no government funding and no financial help from anyone else to go towards books, field trips, stationery or learning materials. Parents are responsible for the cost of everything for their child's home education.

Some have said that this is unfair when they are saving the government thousands of pounds per year by not sending their children to school and they should be entitled to the same amount of funding that every other child receives, whether they are state schooled or home schooled.

Others prefer that the government does not help with funding the cost of home education. If the government funded home-educated children they would certainly want more involvement into how those children were educated and might insist that home-educating parents followed the National Curriculum and adhered to schools' times and terms.

Parents that choose to home educate have to fund their children's education themselves, which is why the majority of home-educating parents also have to work.

Why do it?

Reasons why a parent chooses to home educate their child can include one or many of the following reasons.

Soaring costs of state education

Although a state-funded education should be just that – state funded – a recent study carried out by the Schools Sums index, and compiled by Norwich Union found that the cost of putting a child through a state education is now almost £16,000 and has risen by more than £1,500 in the past two years. It is estimated that parents will pay out a total of £11.4 billion over the course of the next school year – an average of £1,449 per child, per year.

The study found that the cost of transport in getting children to and from school was the biggest expense, followed by lunches and sports kits, which work out more expensive than textbooks.

A survey of more than 1,000 parents of school-aged children found that seven out of ten were worried about how they could afford everything their children needed for school. Added to this, many schools charge for extra curricular activities, and some even ask parents to contribute to a 'school maintenance fund'.

Dissatisfaction with school politics

Many state-funded schools have a board of governors that are involved with every aspect of the school, from meeting targets, to its buildings, staff, parents and pupils. Some parents choose to educate their children at home because they feel that some or many of the aspects of school politics are unfair.

Issues of bullying and abuse at school

In 1999 an anti-bullying policy was enforced in all schools across Britain but despite the government-issued guidelines to all state-funded schools about the need to have zero tolerance to bullying, many parents have found that their complaints and their children's complaints about bullying in school have not been taken seriously.

Bullying UK, a charity who are supported by 26 cross-party MPs, report that they provide 1.2 million people per year with practical advice on bullying. The National Bullying Survey 2006, carried out by the charity revealed that many pupils in UK schools were suffering extreme misery at the hands of classroom bullies.

Many parents have stated that although they have reported issues of bullying the bullies have never been reprimanded. One of the guidelines is, 'if other students at the school are bullying your child, the school has a responsibility to try to sort the problem out.' Many parents feel that this is not the case and the bully has been able to continue to bully their child.

> **Top tip**
>
> If your child has experienced bullying at school encourage him/her to talk about it and use his/her experience in a positive way by creating a project about issues of bullying.
>
> If you require any further information or advice log on to **www.bullying.co.uk**

Dissatisfaction with class sizes

Many parents are understandably worried about the increase in class sizes and although the government have stated that there is now an upper limit of no more than 30 pupils to any one class for children between the ages of five and seven, many older children are being put into classes of up to 34. Some parents feel that this ratio of one teacher per every 30+ pupils is ineffective and inefficient to a child's learning.

Case study: The STAR study

In the mid 1980s a scientific study was carried out by America's most influential educational project, STAR, (Student, Teacher, Achievement, Ratio). STAR was commissioned by the state legislature to carry out a study into class reduction. In its four-year study it found substantial evidence that reducing class size improved a student's academic achievement. This study focussed on 80 schools and included approximately 7,000 Key Stage 3 students from varying backgrounds.

The STAR study found that:

- Smaller classes in the early grades (Key Stage 3) can boost student's academic achievement.
- A class size of no more than 18 students per teacher is required to produce the greatest benefits.
- A programme spanning grades K-3 will produce more benefits than a programme which reaches students in only one or two of the primary grades.
- Minority and low-income students show even greater gains when placed in small classes in the primary grades.
- The experience and preparation of teachers is a critical factor in the success or failure of class size reduction programmes.
- Reducing class size will have little effect without enough classrooms and well-qualified teachers
- Supports, such as professional development for teachers and a rigorous curriculum, enhance the effect of reduced class size on academic achievement.

As more houses and communities are built so the effect is seen in increasing class sizes. It is no coincidence that private or fee-paying schools have lower class sizes and indeed better results. Parents who are paying large fees for their children's education expect their children to be in taught in a manageable class size and most private schools have a limit of no more than 12 pupils per class.

Many people agree that a child cannot learn effectively if a teacher is trying to teach another 29 pupils at the same time and if one pupil does not understand a subject the rest of the class has to wait until he/she does or that child gets overlooked.

A child requires special needs teaching

Although numerous schools are now equipped with special needs teachers, many parents withdraw their children because their children cannot cope with school teaching methods and require learning on a one-to-one basis.

It has been debated that many children have no learning difficulties at all before starting school, but are then diagnosed as have difficulties in reading, learning and behavioural problems. When a child labelled as such is taken out of the school, any problems seem to disappear. One reason for this is believed to be because they can learn at their own pace and have one-to-one teaching. Often children who have been removed from school and then returned to school when they are older do so successfully without any need for a special needs teacher.

It has also been argued that because state-funded schools receive additional funding for children with special needs, children who perhaps learn at a slightly slower pace to other children have been registered as being a child with special needs.

Children who might appear to be slower at learning to read might also be very academic. As I keep saying, every child is unique and just because a child doesn't match up to the average statistics set by the government, does not mean that that child is stupid. All it really means is that that child needs one-to-one teaching, which is what home education is all about.

Case study: Coping with dyslexia

There are many parents of children with dyslexia and dyspraxia who have had no choice but to educate their children at home because they have found that the state school system does not have the time or the resources to dedicate to the needs of their child. The sportsman, Kenny Logan once said of his dyslexia: 'I was a thick, farmer's son all through my schooling. I was made to feel small and stupid and I had a knot in my stomach on the school bus going in every day. I got away with it through confidence, but I had the reading age of seven when I left school.' When Kenny signed for London rugby club, the Wasps, he said, 'I wasn't scared about playing international rugby, just about filling in the gas bill. I used to send the forms back to my mum to fill in for me.'

Unhappiness with the National Curriculum

The National Curriculum was introduced into the UK under the Education Reform Act 1988. It was decided by the government that all state-funded school students, both in primary and secondary schools, were to be taught the same basic curriculum of education across the board. This enabled all Local Authorities to have a common curriculum and to ensure that all state-school students were being taught the same subjects all over the country.

We now also have 68 targets for toddlers, dubbed the 'nappy curriculum' intended as guidelines for pre-school children.

Independent or private schools do not have to follow the National Curriculum and therefore have a greater advantage as to what subjects a student can study.

The issue of standardizing what a child can and cannot learn is one of the reasons many parents choose to educate their children themselves. A child's learning is very limited when they are only allowed to study a limited number of subjects and to a certain level. For those children who absorb information at a faster rate, limited learning can lead them to boredom in the classroom. For those children who perhaps excel in practical learning, the prospect of academic subjects can often leave them flagging behind in a class.

No two children are alike; some love maths, but find English literature boring. Others prefer practical subjects such as woodwork or cookery. Some children love nothing more than to spend hours drawing and painting. Whilst it is a good idea for all children to have a good basic education in different subjects, and this is how the National Curriculum was designed, many parents argue that if a child has tried a subject and has no interest in it, why should they have to continue learning that subject?

Many home-educating parents also feel that the subjects on the National Curriculum are too limited. Home-educated children have more choice in what they want to study than the standard set of subjects that are available in the National Curriculum. If a child shows an interest in say, husbandry he/she can study that subject by means of staying on a farm, starting a smallholding or studying an online course on the subject. There is no opportunity to do this at school.

Added to this, because lessons within the National Curriculum are divided up into lesson plans, the amount of information a child can study on one subject is often limited to one or two half-hour lessons a week. A home-educated child can study a subject in more depth than is possible at school. One of my daughters spent six months studying the works of Shakespeare and still keeps adding to her project.

If a child wants to learn a musical instrument at school they are limited to one hour per week. I know a home-educated child who not only learned to play the electric guitar in three months, but has also set up his own recording studio, has his own band and is well on his way to getting his first recording deal and he's only 14 years old.

Another home-educated child I tutored in journalism spent six months studying the course I designed and is already being commissioned to write articles by magazines. We will discuss more about learning styles later in the book.

> **Top tip**
>
> You can mix and match subjects which you and your child want to learn by studying some subjects of the National Curriculum and combining them with other more vocational subjects for an all-round education.

Religious reasons

Many parents, particularly in America, choose to teach their children from home because of religious reasons. Some of the schools in the UK are Church of England schools and although nowadays they have to make their pupils aware of other religions and often run projects on different cultures, they are primarily a C of E school and religious studies and celebrations will centre around that religion.

Other schools, particularly inner city schools, are multicultural and try to encompass a range of different cultures and religions into their lessons. However, some parents feel that if their children are from a specific practising religion, this should be focussed on more in their day-to-day learning.

Unless a school focuses purely on one single religion and only allows pupils of that religion to attend, some parents feel that they have no other option than to educate their children themselves. One solution to this that has recently been highlighted in the press is that parents who belong to a particular religion have banded together and set up their own small, private schools, enabling their children to continue learning, first hand, about their own culture and religion.

Geographical area

Another reason why some parents choose home education for their children is because of geographical problems. Some children live too far away from a school to be able to attend; others have discovered that they have not been given their choice of a school local to them, resulting in their children having to travel miles every day just to get to school. Some parents have found that the school they want their children to go to is out of their catchment area and for whatever reason they cannot move to that area.

The problem of the increase of residential properties in certain areas has forced some parents to be faced with no alternative but to educate their children themselves. Developers seem to forget that an increase of family homes equals more children in that particular area who will need places at the local school. If the local school is already full, the parents of those children need to find an alternative form of education.

We already have a shortage of good teaching staff within our schools and fewer people are joining the education sector due to poor working conditions and bad pay. State-funded schools, particularly those that are in rural areas, are being closed in favour of schools merging within an area. This results in children who previously attended a school close to their home being told that they must now attend a school that is further away, and because we have fewer teachers, class sizes and school numbers in general are increasing as a result of it.

Problems with teaching staff

I applaud anyone who is faced with the difficult task of trying to keep 30 children interested in a topic and most teachers that I know are hard-working, kind and have the children's best interests at heart. However, there are some parents that feel that their children have been picked on or treated unfairly by the teaching staff and this has led them to take their child out of school.

It sounds like something out of the Dark Ages but I have heard stories of children being made to stand up in front of a class and being made an example of because they have forgotten homework or perhaps because they mistakenly completed the wrong exercise or read the wrong chapter. As parents we tell our children that in order to gain respect you should give respect but this should work both ways. We would never tolerate being humiliated in front of 30 other people and we should not expect or allow our children to either. Teachers are supposed to teach, not abuse their power by adopting an authoritarian attitude to the children in their care. I'm not saying that all teachers lack skills in this department, but there may be some that may benefit from additional training in communication skills and in managing problematic situations.

Freedom in learning

Many parents want their children to have as much freedom as possible in their lives and find that designated school hours, term times and standard lessons all restrict them learning what and when they want to learn.

A number of home-educating families have taken advantage of the fact that they are not tied to the school system by spending their time travelling the world with their children. One family of five bought an old bus, renovated it so that they could live in it and set off to travel the world. What better way for their children to get a hands-on education? Their geography, history, culture and religion lessons have been literally learned at first hand.

As mentioned within the limitations of learning the National Curriculum, some children will naturally excel in some subjects and less in others. It is widely believed that we learn subjects that we love at a faster rate than subjects that we feel less drawn to. As adults, if we choose to go to college or night school we do so because we want to learn a subject – a subject that we choose, not one that we are being forced to learn. Children learn in the same way and many will agree that if we allowed our children to study the subjects that they were truly interested in, they would excel in those subjects, rather than waste time studying something they had no interest in.

Obviously a state-funded school can't adhere to every child's choice of subjects, which is why they have a standardized curriculum and which is also why if children show an interest in

e.g. Summerhill

gypsy

something outside of the National Curriculum, they usually have to study that subject privately out of school hours.

Term times and timetables

As any parent who has ever tried to arrange a family holiday during term times will testify, it is not an easy task to get permission from the school to take their child out of classes for a holiday. Added to this is the fact that resorts bump up the price of holidays as soon as the schools break up, meaning that the costs of a family holiday soar and families with school children pay a higher premium because they are not allowed to take their children out of school.

When you home educate your child you can take your holiday whenever you wish to and whilst this is not the single reason why many parents home school their children, it is certainly a bonus, as is the fact that you don't have to buy school uniforms or stick to the half-hour slots of learning a subject. If your child wishes to spend a whole week on studying an art project, he/she can. If he wants to study paleontology for a year, he can do that too!

It's your choice

As you can see, there are a variety of reasons why parents and children choose home education over state-funded school. Obviously it is not something that suits every child or every family, just as conventional school does not suit every child. Home educating a child is a time-consuming task to take on and parents have to be committed to it in order for it to work. You can't, for instance, leave your child alone to get on with reading a book while you pop out to work for a few hours!

Studies into children who have been home educated have shown that they are better equipped to deal with a variety of situations in life and have better life skills than children who have been educated at school because they have been allowed to make their own decisions and experience life outside of the school gates at a younger age than those of their peers.

It can be

Case studies: Quotes from parents and children in home education

'I can confidently say that I would never have considered home schooling without the various factors that gradually pushed us in that direction. Firstly, we are planning to move house early next year, and uprooting my daughter from school just six months or so after settling her in felt unreasonable. Secondly, we are expecting a new baby (any day now!), and we felt it would be hard on our daughter to be going off to school while it was still all feeling so new, while the rest of the family were at home busily bonding and getting to know each other. Those two factors, combined with our general feeling that kids in this country start school way too young and that there's no rush to get them into formal education, meant that home education became a very attractive option for us.

This feeling grew and grew over the year leading up to September when my daughter was due to start school, and as I continued with my Steiner course for parents and carers I felt increasingly protective of my daughter, wanting to extend her time of play and family.

I then decided to get a whole bag full of books about home education, and slowly, slowly, I came to accept that that was what we were going to do. For a long time I've continued to explain it to others using the first two reasons that I described, above, i.e. house move and new baby. But as more and more parents share with me their concerns about kids starting school so young, etc, I feel more and more confident in stating that my daughter is not at school because we are home schooling.

In some ways it's very simple, as of course it's just a continuation of the life we were living anyway, just with more awareness – on my part – of picking up on my daughter's interests, and pursuing topics that she brings up. What I've found hard, so far, is helping her be OK with all her friends going to school while she doesn't. Of course, she definitely enjoys most of the things we do at home (today we went apple picking at a community orchard nearby), but school still holds an appeal to her, as she's never been. I don't feel committed to home education in the long term, but I do feel increasingly inspired by it all, and very, very sure that we have made the right decision. If we do end up moving house, we will be near to a Steiner school (see page 154), and may well send her there, although by then we may be home ed pros, and decide to stick with that instead!'

Sarah, home educator to Callie, four

'My children are more relaxed and much happier now that they are home schooled. They ask questions and if I don't know the answer we find out together. They have friends who are both home educated and school educated but home schooling works well for my three, they're having a ball!'

Liz, home educator of three years to Amy, 15, Holly, eight and Josh, five

'My daughter, Jennifer, was very unhappy at school and we tried everything. We even changed schools twice, but she was still unhappy and was always making up excuses not to go. School just didn't suit her. Since we have been educating her at home she has come on in leaps and bounds. It's the best decision we have taken for her and she is now taking her GSCE exams a year earlier than she would have done at school.'

Amanda, home educator of four years to Jennifer, 14

'I hated school. I didn't like the way the teacher always thought she knew best and she didn't like it when one time I pointed out that she was wrong about something and sent me to the headmaster's office for being cheeky. I wasn't. I was just telling her that she was wrong. What kind of teacher is that? I've been home educated for three years now and I love it. My passion is sports and in particular cricket. Being home educated means that I can concentrate more on my sports instead of reciting my nine times table over and over again, which I knew anyway. I much prefer being at home.'

Jack, aged 11, home schooled for three years

What the experts say

An academic study carried out between 1996 and 1998 at the Institute of Education, University of London, argues that home education is a viable alternative to school. The authors of this study, Alan Thomas, a visiting fellow in the institute's department of psychology and human development and Harriet Pattison, a research associate, state in their book, *How Children Learn at Home*, that informal learning at home is an astonishingly efficient way to learn and is as good if not better than school for many children.

Thomas and Pattison interviewed and observed the families of more than 70 home-educated children from the UK, Ireland, Australia and Canada. They discovered that these children absorbed information by mainly doing nothing more than having conversations, exploring and through self-learning. They also acknowledged that despite the fact that the parents of these children were not teachers or academics this did not hinder the children's learning.

The authors were amazed at how adaptable the children were and at the different methods of learning: one child learned maths and weights and measures through the simple process of practical learning when helping with the cooking and shopping every week – showing that learning maths can be gained by everyday life skills.

Thomas and Pattison argue that as a society we assume that a formal education needs to take over parental teaching beyond the age of five and yet there is no evidence to suggest that this is any better. They also put to bed the argument of formal education as they found that an informal education is just as good a preparation as any for college, university or private educational course.

Key points

- There is no single reason why parents choose to educate their children at home. Reasons are many and varied.
- Like all of us, children are unique and should be treated like individuals.
- Studies into home education have shown that the education they receive is as good if not better than the school system.

Social class

03

the evidence base

In this chapter you will learn:
- what research says about home education
- about the social and psychological effects of home education
- about further education options.

Those who know how to think need no teachers.

Mahatma Gandhi

Recent research by Dr Rothermel

There have been many studies into how effective home education is, more so in America where home schooling is proving to be a very popular alternative to a state education.

In 2002, Paula Rothermel of the University of Durham set about exploring the aims and practices of home-educating families from different social backgrounds in the UK. Her research involved questioning 419 home-educating families with children aged 11 years and under. The aim of the research was to gain an understanding of home education and it was the first UK study to involve children educated from home using diverse methods. Dr Rothermel has kindly provided the following section which details and summarizes her research findings:

'Very much at odds with the standard view of how children should *Learn* are the findings by me, Educational Psychologist Dr Rothermel of the University of Durham. I found that children who are educated at home during their primary years perform at least as well as schoolchildren even where their parents have little formal education beyond school. What this tells us is that the added value of school, over and above parental input, is perhaps not as significant as often thought. I further found that home-educated children from working class families excelled over their middle class peers. This important finding suggests that the general assumption that children from poorer backgrounds are not going to do well, may be a school effect rather than one of class. This hypothesis is further supported by the 2003 research by Professor Charles Desforges with Alberto Abouchaar and that of Professor Kathy Sylva (also in 2003) whose research shows that after all other factors are accounted for parental involvement is the most important factor in children's attainment.

Whilst the findings relate to home-educated children, they also provide the insight into what parents can achieve in terms of helping develop their children's potential. When learning outside the formality of school it appears that children absorb their knowledge gradually by virtue of informal repetition and assimilation through everyday learning involving the natural

?

Paragraph (1)

Advantages

process of dialogue and exploration. This style of acquiring information has been found by researchers to be more readily retained than that acquired didactically at school. Eminent Child Psychologist, Professor Annette Karmiloff-Smith has described the way in which children take on board information from the external world, re-organizing it internally and combining it through conflict and/or agreement with previously internalized knowledge, eventually attaining mastery over the situation. She described this process as 'representational re-description' and it is this process that fits so well with the idea that parents are well placed to support their children's personalized learning.

So what did I actually do? Well, I started with an open book, planning simply to open a window on home education. I came from the perspective of having no prior knowledge of home education; I had no children at the outset of my research and held no pre-conceptions about what I might find. Starting initially with a plan to survey as many home educators as possible I was overwhelmed with over 1,000 responses of which a smaller sample were analyzed for my research. Fascinated by home educators descriptions, I decided to broaden the study to include in-depth interviews and combine this with quantitative analysis by inviting families to participate in a programme of academic, social and psychological assessments with children aged up to 11 years of age. Whilst the sample was in effect self-selecting, it is important to note that participants in the original social survey had no idea that they would be invited to join in with the assessment programme. Families were selected for the assessments strictly on the basis of the ages of their children and all children in each of the relevant age groups were invited to participate. Only one family declined the invitation. This study remains the largest and most important of its kind, including as it did, a very broad section of the home-educating community. Access is always a problem with home education and my original survey was distributed through a number of home-educating organizations as well as religious groups, Local Authorities and Internet sites.'

Overview of Dr Rothermel's study

In analyzing the questionnaire returns and interviews conducted, Dr Rothermel focussed her findings under a number of headings:

The pattern of home education, the motivation and the expectation

From the sample, about 50 per cent of the home-educated children had been home educated from birth and about 50 per cent had been withdrawn from school. A common pattern was that once a child was withdrawn, subsequent children, either pre-school aged or not yet born, would be home educated from the outset. Rothermel found that about half the home-educating families did so because of their poor experience with schools. The other half made the decision based on family lifestyle. However, whilst dissatisfaction with school may have been a true motivation for many, this was partnered with a growing sense of choice. Home education, once initiated, became a lifestyle decision; initial motivations were sidelined as families found other benefits. About half the home educators found home education not as they expected. It was either more fun, more demanding or both. Nevertheless, few parents made negative comments about home educating.

National Curriculum

Parents, whether becoming more or less formal over time, adapted to their children's needs. Confident parents tended to shun the National Curriculum whilst those who were less confident either followed, or were at least mindful of it.

'Homework'

The most time spent by families on 'formal' education lasted no more than 2–3 hours a day. Families did not consider maths and science to be problems and once need outstripped family knowledge, children tended to join further education colleges or other formal lessons, for example, online courses. Over half the families said that they made use of 'learning support' in the form of clubs and classes such as football, trampolining, dance, music etc.

Assessment

Almost half of the respondents did not assess their children and of those that did a third reported that they used only informal assessment such as discussion and observation.

What families valued

The space to develop non-academic intelligences was an advantage of home education. There was also more room for family activities, discussion and spontaneity. Respondents believed that listening to their children, sharing experiences and involving the children in everyday responsibilities contributed to the children's education and growth in a way that school could not.

Isolation within the community

In terms of fellowship, families often felt isolated within their communities although this was not of their choosing. Whilst some families succumbed to the pressure, for most this was not enough reason to adopt or re-adopt the school ethos.

Alienation from the wider community

Families found they were constantly questioned in the street and their children were asked questions about their maths and reading skills. In the questionnaires, this constant questioning and related feeling of being different was given as the main disadvantage of home education. There was, however, evidence from the interviews of increasing acceptance within the community.

Friends

The questionnaire responses showed that almost one-fifth of families believed their children would suffer if the parents did not find friends for them, although this was very much a parental issue and not one echoed by the children during the interviews. When the children wanted company they mostly felt able to choose to spend time with, all or either, home-educated friends, school friends and siblings. However, location and transport could bring limitations.

Searching for something

There was a sense of families searching out an ideal that was not home and not school but some midway alternative.

Working to the school year

Without school 'pegs' upon which to organize days some families felt a little lost. However, in a broader sense, many families found themselves working to the school year. Children had friends in school and this meant completing their activities in time to meet with their school friends. Other reasons for this were that many children were involved with after-school groups, home educators sometimes used buildings available only during term time to meet up in. Home educators also made use of swimming pools, museums, libraries etc. during school hours to avoid the crowds.

Change over time

Families underwent a metamorphosis once they started to home educate. Parents often learned in tandem with their children. They often re-arranged their working lives so that they could both share the children. Fathers were more involved than the norm. Flexibility and fluidity characterized families as they searched for and found what suited them. Very 'normal' families, once home educating, often underwent a metamorphosis, sometimes quite radically, as a result of their decision and their mixing with other home educators.

Adapting to child-centred learning

This research found, as had Alan Thomas in 1998, that the children were influential in discreetly manoeuvring their learning to suit themselves. Whether families started off formally or less formally in terms of learning patterns, they all adjusted to a style that suited their children. This outcome was usually the converse of what parents expected.

The joy of home educating

The questionnaire results revealed that over one-third of parents found home educating far more fun than they could have imagined. The interviews found that more often than not, home educating was a lifestyle decision. It was a choice about how to live far more than a statement about schooling. Families found they talked about things that mattered, describing themselves as, 'doing what we want, when we want'. Parents believed their children were developing naturally and the families involved clearly valued their closeness. There was little evidence of the sibling rivalry so often accepted as 'normal'.

The assessment programme

Children aged between four and five years old were tested twice over a 'school' year.

The PIPS baseline assessment data indicated that 64 per cent of the children scored over 75 per cent on the assessment, nationally just 5.1 per cent of children scored over 75 per cent. 'End of Reception year' data suggested that the children's progress over the period was less than that associated with school children during their reception year. This observation, however, was offset by the home-educated children's high baseline scores. Children from the lower end of the socio-economic class scale significantly outscored those from the upper spectrum of the scale. Interestingly, there were no score differences between families who owned and did not own a television. Children from religious families did not score significantly differently from those children from more secular families at the start of Reception although by the end of Reception the score difference was significant.

The results from the literacy assessments with slightly older children were also fascinating. Children's scores can be described as falling into certain 'bands'. Normally, we expect to find 16 per cent of children in the top band. Percentages of home-educated children within this score band for literature were as follows:

> 94 per cent of six year olds
> 77.4 per cent of seven year olds
> 73.3 per cent of eight year olds
> 82.3 per cent of ten year olds

Social and psychological data

The final set of results from Dr Rothermel's research looked at social and psychological data. The purpose of these assessments was to establish whether home-educated children experienced social or behavioural problems. Overall, the results confirmed that home-educated children were socially adept and did not display behavioural problems above the norm although there were some problems noted when the home-educated children needed to make or received complaints. The children were, perhaps, less conversant with negative opinions than those in the general population.

Dr Rothermel suggested that her work opened the way for further discussion within the main areas as follows:

1 The research found that the baseline assessments were not useful in finding out about the home-educated children because these tests were unable to assess the children's individual and idiosyncratic learning experiences and their high scores masked their diverse skills.

2 Poverty was not an indicator of poor academic outcomes where parents, whatever their situation, were committed to their children.

3 The children may have performed so well because they were not under pressure when taking these tests.

4 Home education, insofar as these tests are concerned, was far more successful and efficient than even the parents anticipated.

5 There was evidence of metacognitive thought – the children were aware of their limitations.

6 Learning in families was negotiated and differentiated for each child.

7 Observations made during the testing programme showed just how inappropriate it was to use school style measures on home-educated children. For Local Authorities monitoring home education, the proposition that home-educated children should not be measured by criteria devised for school children may assist in the drive to formulate policies for alternative assessment. The tests gave no insight into the extent of these children's learning. The research found that the children's learning was best described as a multidirectional and mutlilayered model, and that such a model was not provided for by standard tests.

8 The findings from the psychosocial data have an impact on how Local Authorities, Court Welfare and Social Services view home-educated children. If such agencies adopt 'norms' by which to judge such children, they will almost invariably find these children to be outside the 'norm'. What is desirable behaviour from a schoolchild is very different from what is deemed desirable behaviour from a home-educated child.

Paula Rothermel concludes by saying that overall, the home-educated children demonstrated high levels of attainment and good social skills. Common to all families was their flexible approach. The children benefited from parental attention and the freedom to develop their skills at their own pace. Families enjoyed strong bonds and parents were committed to providing a nurturing environment for their children.

© Dr P. Rothermel, 2008

> **Top tip**
>
> To read Dr Paula Rothermel's full study into home education, visit her website at **www.paularothermel.co.uk**

Research into levels of achievement

Studies carried out by other educational experts have found that the reasons why parents choose to educate their children from home include:

- bullying by a teacher and/or other pupils (this was the highest score of 'other reasons')
- dyslexia and dyspraxia
- asperger's and autism
- hyperactivity, ADD and ADHD
- exceptional ability/a gifted child
- specific learning problems
- health problems
- disability
- school phobia
- religious reasons
- the National Curriculum
- the philosophy of home education
- dissatisfaction with school and/or the education system
- parents wishing to be part of their children's education
- the child's choice
- the belief that children should not be institutionalized.

American research

National Home Education Research Institute

Home education or home schooling as it is sometimes known is much more accepted in the United States of America. In 2003, the Home School Legal Defense Association commissioned the largest research survey to date of adults that had been educated at home. The survey was conducted by Dr Brian Ray of the National Home Education Research Institute and surveyed over 7,300 adults who had been home schooled. Over 5,000 of these had been home educated for at least seven years. Two important points came from this research, one concerning further education and the other employment.

The study wanted to investigate whether being home educated would hinder a child's chances of going to college and found that the end of formal home schooling was not the end of the educational road for most. Over 74 per cent of home-educated adults, aged between 18 and 24, took college level courses, compared to 46 per cent of the general population in the US. Thus proving that home education is not an obstacle if a child wishes to go on to further education.

Not surprisingly, Dr Ray's study found that since home education is fairly common in the US, home-educated adults are employed in a variety of occupations. For parents who wonder whether they are doing the right thing by home schooling their children, it is encouraging to know that 95 per cent of adults who were educated at home are in full-time employment and are also glad that they were home schooled. The results of Dr Ray's research defused the long-held beliefs that home education was wrong for a child and proved that home schooling produces successful adults, who are actively involved in their communities.

Strengths of Their Own: Home Schoolers Across America

In 1997, a study of 5,402 home-educated students from 1,657 families was released. It was entitled, 'Strengths of Their Own: Home Schoolers Across America'. The study demonstrated that home schoolers, on average, out-performed their counterparts in the public schools by 30–7 per cent in all subjects. Another significant finding when analyzing the data for eighth graders was the evidence that home schoolers who are home schooled for two or more years scored substantially higher than students who have been home schooled for one year or less.

This was confirmed in another study by Dr Lawrence Rudner. He found that of 20,760 home-schooled students those who had been educated from home for all their school-aged years had the highest academic achievement. This was especially apparent in the higher grades.

Another important finding of 'Strengths of Their Own' was that the race of the student did not make any difference. There was no significant difference between minority and white home-schooled students. In the state schools, however, there is a sharp contrast. White, public school, eighth grade students nationally scored 58 per cent in maths and 57 per cent in reading. Black, eighth grade students on the other hand scored on average 24 per cent in maths and 28 per cent in reading. These findings show that when parents, regardless of race, commit themselves to make the necessary sacrifices and tutor their children at home, almost all obstacles present in other school systems disappear.

Another obstacle that seems to be overcome in home education is the need to spend a great deal of money in order to have a good education. In 'Strengths of Their Own' the average cost per home-educated student is £250 while the average cost per state-school student is £3,325. Yet the home-educated children in this study averaged 85 per cent while the public school students averaged 50 per cent on nationally standardized achievement tests.

The message in Dr Ray's study found that more money does not result in a better education. There is no positive correlation between money spent on education and student performance. State-funded school advocates could re-focus their emphasis if they learned this lesson. Loving and caring parents are what matters. Money can never replace simple, hard work.

The last significant statistic from the 'Strengths of Their Own' study regards the effect of government regulation on home education. Dr. Brian Ray compared the impact of government regulation on the academic performance of home-educated students and he found no positive connection. In other words, whether a state had a high degree of regulation (for example curriculum approval, teacher qualifications, testing, home visits) or a state had no regulation for home-educators, the home-schooled students in both categories of states performed the same. The students all scored on the average in the 86th percentile regardless of state regulation.

This material was reproduced with the kind permission of the Home School Legal Defence Association (www.hslda.org).

National Centre for Home Education
In a study released by the National Centre for Home Education in 1994, according to tests of 16,311 home-educated children, from all 50 states, the nationwide average for home-educated students is 77 per cent for the basic skills. In reading, home-educated children attained a 79 per cent success rate.

A further study conducted by the National Centre for Home Education in South Carolina surveyed 65 home-educated students and found that the average scores on the Comprehensive Test of Basic Skills were 30 per cent higher than national state school averages. In maths, 92 per cent of the home-educated students scored above grade level, and 93 per cent of the home-educated students were at or above grade level in reading.

Home School Legal Defense Association
In 1991, a survey of standardized test scores was performed by the Home School Legal Defense Association in co-operation with the Psychological Corporation, which publishes the Stanford Achievement Test. The study involved the administering of the Stanford Achievement Test (8th Edition, Form J) to 5,124 home-schooled students. These students represented all 50 states and their grades. This testing was administered in Spring 1991 under controlled test conditions in accordance with the test publisher's standards. All test

administers were screened, trained and approved to the publisher's requirements. All tests were machine-scored by the Psychological Corporation.

These combined scores of the 5,124 home schoolers in reading, maths, language and arts ranked between 18 and 28 per cent above the state school averages. The home-educated students scored better than state-schooled children in every test presented to them.

Top tip

Studies into home-educated children have shown that they perform as well if not better than school-educated children.

Research into further education

Something that is always on a home-educating parent's mind is whether or not being home educated will have an adverse affect on their child gaining access to college or a university.

In 2003, Trevena Whitbread (BA Hons), home educator to her twins, researched whether or not it was more difficult for home-educated children to get into a British college or university. This was something that had not been researched before and Trevena interviewed six young people who were home educated. Her studies found that none of them had any difficulties with the admissions departments in gaining access to college or university.

Trevena's study found that far from home education being a deterrent to accessing college or university, it seems to be regarded as a positive asset. Out of the six students interviewed by Trevena, some said that they had to push to get where they wanted to go, whilst for others it was easier, but they all agreed that they were glad that they had been educated at home and have found it to be a positive experience. None of the interviewees reported having any difficulties fitting into their peer groups when returning to a mainstream education and all were able to relate well to their tutors.

Trevena's investigation into home education found that regardless of their age, children educated at home learnt because they want to learn about what was going on around them, rather than being ordered to learn and being told what they could and could not learn. She argued that home education was a good preparation for children and young people and a good stepping stone to college and university should they choose that path. The study also demonstrated that traditional school students tended to sit their exams without any clue of what they want to do later in life. However, because home-educated children had been given more freedom in what they wished to learn about, they often knew what they wanted to do as a career and would study the necessary qualifications required. This demonstrates a far more direct way of dealing with qualifications – simply going and getting exactly what is needed instead of young people spending years getting qualifications they may never need or use, or that in 20 or 30 years are completely out of date.

Trevena's study revealed that people that are educated at home were less prone to drugs, heavy drinking, petty crime or vandalism and tended to be emotionally intelligent and socially mature. They were rarely unemployed and did well if they went on to university. There was no evidence that the youngsters who wanted to go on to college or university experienced any difficulties in doing so and were judged on their own performance and merit, rather than their lack of academic qualifications.

Trevena found that what struck her most about home-educated children and young people was their self-motivation and their ability to become lifelong learners. They had been encouraged by their parents to self learn which in turn led them to make choices relevant to their individual interests, rather than following the herd and choosing subject/careers that simply matched those of their peers.

This study comes as welcome news to all parents who have considered home education but have worried about qualifications and progression into higher education and the career pathway.

Key points

- Studies of home-educated children have shown that child-centered learning promotes improved performance in comparison to school-educated children.
- In general home-educated children score above average in standard school tests.
- There is no evidence that home-educated children are at a disadvantage if they wish to go on to college or university.

04

questions and queries

What we want to see is the child in pursuit of knowledge, not knowledge in pursuit of the child.

George Bernard Shaw

Frequently asked questions

Is it really legal to educate my child from home?

Apart from a handful of states and countries, yes, it is legal to educate your child from home. People forget that years ago a home education was once considered to be a privilege. It was only the wealthy who could afford to home school their children. All other children either never went to school or attended a state-funded school.

For younger children it is the most natural thing to learn from their parents. Studies have proved that children learn a subject better in their own environment and under their own steam than if they were taught the same subject in a classroom at school.

As long as you provide your child with an education that is adequate to his/her learning ability and age, you have nothing to worry about.

My child is already registered at a school, can I still home educate?

Yes, you can. If your child is already registered at a school, you can still legally educate your child, so long as you de-register that child from that school. We will look more at this in Chapter 05. You cannot legally educate your child from home if your child is still registered with a school. However, occasionally some schools will allow flexi-learning so that a child can learn some lessons at home and others at school such as sports, or if your child is a child actor.

Can I start home education whenever I want?

Yes you can. You do not have to start at the beginning of a new year or even a new term. There are no rules about the time that you de-register a child from school so long as you do it before you begin your home education.

Once I start home education, do I have to continue teaching my child from home forever?

No. There are no set rules to say that once you de-register your child from school and begin teaching from home that your child has to continue learning from home until they are 16. Some home educators have taught their children during their younger years and then sent them into the school system when they are older; others have taken their children out of school for the period of time whilst they go travelling and then re-register them back into school when they return. For some, the idea of home schooling at first seems appealing, but for various reasons discover it is not for them. Others might want to try it for a set period of time after which they may then decide they prefer the structure of the state school system.

It doesn't matter if you start home schooling and decide it's not for you. Children can chop and change their minds like the weather and whilst it's great to not have to get up early in the morning to catch the bus and then spend six hours a day in a stuffy classroom, the novelty of learning at home can sometimes wear off.

Depending on the area you live in, many older children that have been educated at home are allowed to attend their local college from the age of 14, particularly if they wish to take GCSEs or a course in a specific subject. Check with your Local Authority and local college to see if they accept under 16s.

Do I have to keep to the school hours or school syllabus?

No, you do not have to keep to school hours. You can set the hours you want for the times your child/children study to fit in with your work and family commitments. Your children do not have to stick to the set six hours a day that they would do at school, nor do they have to follow any specific timetable or lesson times.

We will cover learning styles in more depth later, but you are under no obligation to teach your child the same syllabus that they teach in schools. Just because the majority of school-aged children are learning the same subject to the same level, it does not mean that your child/children have to. If you were going to college you wouldn't study every subject that that college offers, would you? You would choose a subject that you are interested in learning and study it thoroughly.

Remember, every child is unique and their choice of learning should also be unique. You may notice that your child is most alert for the first three hours of the morning and is eager to learn then, but is not so eager during the afternoon. That is fine, stick to studying a subject in the morning and have the afternoon free to play sports, go out walking or shopping together.

My youngest daughter who is six years old works best in half hour bursts. We will read or play a maths game for half an hour and then she will get itchy feet and will want to go out on the trampoline for ten minutes. This is fine as she's still learning but she also knows when she needs a break. We then change subjects for another half an hour and do something like computer work.

By comparison, our eldest daughter is a night owl and works best during the evening and into the night. To start with, many home-schooling parents try to stick with the traditional hours of schooling, but more often than not this will change as your children let you know when they are at their most productive.

I have three children of different ages, how can I possibly teach them all?

I also have three children of differing ages – one is 15, the next is 12 and the youngest is six. Obviously they all have different interests and abilities to learn, so they can't possibly all be interested in any one subject and at the same level.

You will find that with older children they will soon tell you what they want to learn about and with the help of computers and libraries they will happily set their own timetable and study plans and learn at their own pace and on their own.

Younger children need more guidance than their older siblings, but I and many other home-schooling parents have found that younger children are naturally led by their older siblings. This is why the Montessori learning system works so well. Montessori classes have children of all ages in their classes and the learning system is one where the child decides what he or she wants to learn and when. We will discuss learning styles and techniques in Chapter 06.

What will people think of me if I home educate my children?

Although I know after four years that home education is the best thing we have ever done for our children, there are still days when I dread the nosey cashier in the supermarket and the obligatory question every one of them asks me and my children; 'No school today, dears?' or 'In-service day today?'

When I'm feeling strong and confident I proudly stand tall and say, 'No, my children are home schooled.' I have to feel strong and confident because I then have to explain that, yes, it is legal and no, they are not missing out and no, I am not a qualified teacher and yes, they do study maths and...

Other days when I'm in a hurry, or I'm not feeling up to justifying to the world as to why I don't send my children off to school everyday, like the majority of other parents in the county, I simply tell them that they have a dental appointment.

Occasionally I will fight my corner when they say things like, 'What do they do all day?' and I tend to question them as to whether they actually know what their children are doing all day? Or the big debate that starts with, 'What about exams?' which is usually answered (only if I'm feeling strong, confident and somewhat pedantic) with something along the lines of, 'The state-funded schools that your children attend will take exams that are set by the government and are not necessarily a sign of a child's ability to do a job.'

I have had people literally refuse to talk to me again the moment they have found out that I home educate my children. I was once invited to a chocolate party where there were a number of part-time teaching assistants among the guests. No sooner had the hostess introduced me and told them that I educate my children from home, they all turned their back on me and wouldn't speak to me for the rest of the evening. I would have got a better reception if I had announced that I had the plague!

By the same token I have also had some wonderful responses from other people who are more open-minded and more accepting to alternative lifestyles than some teaching assistants. Even my daughter's ex-headmaster congratulated us on our endeavours and told me that he knew that not all children were suited to a state-school education.

The reason why some people are bigoted about home schooling is because they either do not understand that it is a legal alternative to state-funded education or they are blinkered and unable to contemplate that a child can learn as well if not better than a child at school. In some cases they are jealous that they can't or won't provide their own children with this opportunity. Interestingly, I'm willing to bet that if you were to say that your child went to a private school, which theoretically is what they are doing, you would be thought of very highly.

In short, unfortunately, if you do not conform to the majority of what everyone else is doing you are bound to be thought of as a little odd. The only way you can cope with this is to stay away from and ignore those people who are opposed to the way you educate your children and accept that you are doing what you feel is right for you and your family. To be perfectly honest, it really is no one else's business how you educate your children.

I'm not a qualified teacher, so how can I teach?

Neither am I and nor is my husband. You don't have to be a qualified teacher in order to be able to provide a good education for your children. Qualified teachers are only qualified to teach the National Curriculum. If you feel that your children would benefit from following the National Curriculum there is nothing to stop you from buying the required books and learning materials that they provide in schools and teaching your child from the book. Younger children in school will concentrate on being able to read and write effectively and this is relatively easy to do with a combination of early learning books, worksheets and games.

For a lot of families, the whole purpose of being home schooled is to escape from the traditional methods of learning and being given the freedom to learn when and what subjects they want – many of which are not covered within the National Curriculum. You will also find that your children will naturally lean to subjects that they want to know about, so rather than forcing a subject on them that they have no interest in, they will begin to tell you what they want to learn about.

Many home educators (myself included) started out by buying stacks of learning materials and workbooks only for them to remain unopened because their children decided that what they want to learn doesn't match up with what you think they want to learn.

The main ingredient you need if you are going to be a home educator is time. You do not need to know everything. How can you possibly? There are many ways in which you can help your child to learn and you don't need a qualification to do it.

Do I have to employ tutors?

No, you do not have to employ tutors if you don't want to, although some home-educating parents pay for private lessons in subjects that they know nothing about themselves. This might be learning a particular musical instrument or studying a specialized method of computer programming. Very often you will find that other home-educating parents will swap skills with each other and teach each others children.

I know one home-educating mum who is a professor of mathematics and happily offers help with maths to other home-schooled children in return for various lessons ranging from learning the piano to taking French lessons.

There are also many other people who will help you if you ask them: my sister is a businesswoman and provides lessons in business studies to my 15 year old; a friend of ours owns a zoo and will often take our middle daughter off for the day to learn zoology; another friend is a drama and dance teacher who happily coaches our youngest daughter for nothing; and we pay for private piano lessons from a student who is studying music at the local college.

You will often find that people in your locality have a wide range of skills to offer and if you ask for their help, they are often happy to pass on their skills to your children.

Who am I answerable to?

Although you are not answerable to anyone as to how you educate your child, your Local Authority may request to visit you to ensure that your child is receiving an education suitable to his/her age and abilities. Please see page 51 for deregistering your child and page 57 for first contact with the Local Authority.

Does home educating cost a lot of money?

Home educating your child/children can cost as much or as little as you choose. You do not have to be wealthy to offer your child a good education. The most important aspect that you can give them is time and encouragement.

We will discuss learning styles in more depth in Chapter 06, but the way your child learns will determine how much it will cost you to home educate them. If, for example, you intend to copy the school learning style and follow the National Curriculum, you will need to invest in the same books and study materials that the school provides. You might also want to invest in a black/whiteboard, desk, and even a 'school room' so that your lessons are carried out at specific times and in a separate room.

Because we mainly use the autonomous style of learning for our children, the cost of our resources are very low. I buy stationery, folders for projects, pens and pencils and a lot of art supplies, but I no longer buy appropriate Key Stage workbooks unless one of our children specifically asks for it.

Many families don't have any formal lessons and prefer to teach their children by the method of learning from experience. This is a particularly effective option for families who wish to travel for months at a time. Added to this, you do not have to pay out for costs such as a school uniform, pay bus fares or other expenses that you do when your child goes to school.

Is there any government funding?

In short, the answer is no. There is no governmental funding for people that choose to educate their children at home. Children that go to a state-funded school are funded annually by the government for their place in that school. If a parent chooses to send their child to a private school where the freedom of choice in education is more prevalent, the government does not provide any funding for this, as is also the case with home-educated children. A recent report from the Headmasters' and Headmistresses' Conference stated that it is now cheaper to educate a child at a private school than in a state-funded school because despite the huge sums of money the government invest into state education a lot of it never gets close to a child's education and is used up on bureaucracy instead.

Top tip

There is no government funding for home-educators, but there are plenty of free resources available via the Internet, libraries or communities.

Will I still get child benefit?

Yes. Child benefit is payable to all children, whether they go to school or are educated in another way. Just before a child reaches the age of 16, their parents will receive a letter asking whether the child will be continuing their full-time education after their 16th birthday. If your child is going to continue with his/her education from home or at college you should confirm this. Provided that your child has been home educated before the age of 16, the child benefit will continue. The Education Section at the Child Benefit Offices use section DMG11094 – the Decision Makers Guide – to decide whether or not full-time education is taking place.

If a child begins home education after the age of 16, then the rule DMG11093 applies instead. This states that a full-time education course is one where a person attends a recognized educational establishment for more than 12 hours each week.

Many of the child benefit advisors are not fully aware of the rules relating to home-educators and can mislead parents. If you contact them and they tell you that your child benefit has ceased, you should ask to speak to someone in the full-time education section.

What about socialization?

We will cover socialization issues more in Chapter 08, but you should not worry about whether your child will suffer socially just because they are taught at home. There has been a lot of research on this issue showing that rather than suffering, home-educated children are in fact better equipped at dealing with people of all ages and abilities than their school peers.

What about qualifications?

As we discussed in Chapter 03, just because a child is educated at home doesn't mean that he/she can't take formal exams. We will look at this in more depth later in the book, but anyone can enter for an exam as an external student. If your child wishes to study for their GCSEs, or any other exam, they have many options to be able to do this that don't include a classroom and many home-educated children take their exams earlier than school children.

I have a child with special needs, can I still home educate?

Yes, you can still home educate a child with special needs; in fact, children with special needs excel in a one-to-one environment. If your child is registered with a social worker or as a child with special needs at a special needs school you will need to obtain permission from your Local Authority to educate your child from home.

My son only wants to study one subject, is this OK?

Because the National Curriculum was designed to provide a wide range of subjects at a very basic level so that every student could gain an insight into a variety of subjects, there are always going to be subjects that children love studying and others that they'd rather not study. The beauty of home education is that a child will quickly discover what subjects they really enjoy and can spend their time studying just those subjects if they choose.

For example, if your child is passionate about music and shows little interest in learning anything else, this is quite alright. Your child might enjoy learning new languages, this is fine too. I know one 14-year-old boy whose only interest is in computer games and this is the only subject he studies. He is currently working towards a degree in web development and plans to work as a computer programmer when he is older.

The beauty of a home education is that a child can take time to learn a subject that they are interested in for as long as they like. They are not restricted to studying a subject they enjoy for a couple of hours a week. You will generally find that once they realize that they can study what they want, when they want, they will study a subject fully and then move on to something new.

My personal opinion is that as long as your child is able to read, write and understand basic maths then they should be able to choose what they want to study.

Top tip

Ask friends and family to help out, many will have skills that you do not and are usually only too happy to help with your child's learning.

Can my children be seen out and about?

With the new laws on truancy from school it can make it difficult for older children who are home educated to prove that they are indeed home educated and not just playing truant from school if they are out during normal school hours. The Crimes and Disorder Act states that:

'In planning for, and operating, a truancy initiative using the new power it is important to remember that not all children aged 5–16 are registered at school. Children educated outside the school system altogether, for example, by home tuition, might be out and about during the daytime for wholly legitimate reasons, for example visiting a library.

'Local procedures should take account of possible contact with such home-educated children and it should be emphasized that they are not the target group for the new power. The power can only be exercised in relation to registered pupils of compulsory school age absent from school without authority; it does not apply to children who are lawfully educated at home. No further action should be taken where children indicate that they are home educated – unless the constable has reason to doubt that this is the case.'

The charity Education Otherwise issue wallet-size cards that a child can carry with them that explains the Education Laws and states that they are educated at home. Your Local Authority may also have a policy of issuing home-education cards to home-educated children.

There are no rules to stipulate that a child who is educated at home has to remain in their home from 9 a.m. to 3 p.m. I have never been approached by a police or truancy officer and asked why my children are not at school when they are out with me, however, if you ever are, all you have to say is that your child is home educated.

Is home education suitable for everyone?

No, just as school is not suitable for everyone. If you are going to educate your child at home you need to make a commitment to yourself and your child for however long you aim to educate them. Not every parent wants their children at home all day long and not every parent is able to provide an education for their children due to work commitments. Not every child will want to be taught at home because they enjoy going to school. The option of educating your child at home is something that you need to discuss as a family.

> **Top tip**
>
> Sit down with your child and make a list of the pros and cons of home educating. This will prepare you both in advance for what you may encounter.

Key points

- Home-educated children are not limited to what they can learn and will be able to study specific subjects more thoroughly.
- It is not a problem if your child decides he/she doesn't enjoy being home educated.
- You can start home educating whenever you wish.

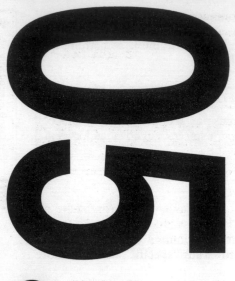

05

de-registration

In this chapter you will learn:
- about the de-registration process
- how to compose letters for de-registering a child
- about your Local Authority.

Thank goodness I was never sent to school; it would have rubbed off some of the originality.

Beatrix Potter

De-registering your child from school

Not all parents are aware that you can legally provide an education other than that provided by a school. Most automatically register their child at the local school from the age of five because they do not realize that home education is an available option.

As I mentioned in Chapter 03, research shows that there are many reasons why parents choose to educate their children at home and you will find that most have tried state education and have been dissatisfied with some aspect of it.

Top tip

Remember: Your child must be educated, but school is not compulsory.

When you register your child at a school, your child is then listed on the admissions register. If you wish to remove your child from that school by law that child has to be de-registered from that school.

In England, when you wish to remove a child from the school register in order to home educate you have to go through what is known as a de-registering process. This is not as scary as it sounds. It simply involves writing to the head teacher or principal of the school – sample letters are included later in this chapter.

All schools are required by law to keep a register of the names of each child that attends that school. Regulation 8 (1)(d) of the Education (Pupil Registration) Regulations 2006 states that a school-aged pupil's name is to be deleted from the admission register if:

'he has ceased to attend the school and the proprietor has received written notification from the parent that the pupil is receiving education otherwise than at school.'

When you write to the head teacher or the principal of the school that your child has been attending some parents feel that they have to justify the reasons why they are withdrawing their child from school. You do not have to justify your reasons to anyone. Just as if you were moving area, you would simply de-register your child from one school in favour of another.

> **Top tip**
> Always keep a record of letters you receive or write with regard to your child's education.

Children with special needs in special schools

Although regulation 8 (1) (d) allows de-registration of a child from a school, this ruling does not apply to children who have been placed in special needs schools by the Local Authority (LA). This does not mean that you are prohibited from removing your child from school, but you will need your LA's permission – this is covered in Regulation 8 (2) in the Education (Pupil Registration) Regulations. It has been said that this is to protect the interests of more vulnerable children and to ensure that their special needs are met. However, this regulation can make it more difficult for parents of children with special needs who feel that their LA are not providing adequate learning to their children.

It has also been noted that by insisting that the LA gives parents consent, making it harder to de-register their child, it could be interpreted as discrimination and prejudice. Section 7 of the 1996 Education Act states that the right to educate a child by school or **otherwise** also applies to children with special needs, therefore it comes as a bit of a contradiction if they are also saying that you have to have the LA's permission in order to de-register your child from a special needs school.

De-registration from a school in Wales

Home education policies are covered under the Welsh Assembly Guidelines for children who live in Wales.

The 1995 Education (Pupil Registration) Regulations detail how the de-registration process works and how a pupil's name must be removed from the admission register of a school.

Regulation 9 (1)(c) states that a pupil of school age should be deleted from the admission register if:

'He has ceased to attend the school and the proprietor has received written notification from the parent that the pupil is receiving education otherwise than at school.'

As with the rules for English children, parents of a child that is registered at a school and who starts home education have to inform the head teacher that they are providing an alternative education. The child will then be removed from the school admissions register.

Parents do not have to inform or gain permission from the Local Authority to home educate. However, as with schools in England, under Regulation 13 (3) the head teacher or principal of the school has an obligation to report the deletion of the pupil's name from the admissions register.

As with schools in England, if a parent with a child that is registered at a special needs school in Wales wishes to de-register their child from a special needs school, they are obliged to have the consent of the LA in order to withdraw their child from the school – this is covered by Regulation 9 (2) of the Education (Pupil Registration) Regulations 1995. However, in Wales this is only considered a helpful measure to help the child and parents have a smooth transition into being home educated and is not intended to be a block against parents' choices.

Despite it being legal, some parents who have tried to de-register their child from school have come across a head teacher who refuses to do so. Do not be put off by this obstruction. A head teacher has no right to refuse to de-register your child from their school – the sample letter later in this chapter makes reference to this, should you encounter this problem.

Top tip

Just as you are not expected to justify to anyone which school you choose to send you child to, you do not have to justify the reasons why you wish to educate your child from home. You do not have to go into any great detail when you contact the school or when the LA contact you – we will discuss how to deal with the LA in Chapter 07.

Sample de-registration letters

Letter to the head teacher requesting them to de-register your child (in England)

[Your Address]

[Head teacher's name]
[School's address]
[Date]

Dear [Name of head teacher]

Re: [Name of child]

We have decided to teach [name of child] at home. Please consider this my notification that [name of child] is to receive "education otherwise than at school" and deregister my child from your school in accordance with the Education (Pupil Registration) Regulation 8 (1) (d) 2006.

Please confirm that you have received this letter and deregistered [name of child] accordingly.

Yours sincerely,

[Your name]

You do not have to go into any great detail as to the reasons why you wish your child to be de-registered and you are not obliged to answer any questions about your child's welfare, your qualifications to teach your child, or how you intend to educate your child. The above letter is enough.

Letter to the governors should the head teacher refuse to de-register your child from their school (in England)

This letter should be sent to the chair of governors of the school if you are faced with a head teacher that is reluctant to de-register your child from school.

[Chair of Governors]

[School's address]

[Date]

Dear [Chair of Governors]

Re: [Name of child. Date of birth]

On [date] I/we wrote to the head teacher, [head teacher's name], at [name of school] to deregister [name of child] from [name of school] in accordance with the Education (Pupil Registration) Regulation 8 2006 because we wish to take responsibility for [child's name]'s education ourselves.

Regulation 8 (1) (d) 2006 states that a child is to be deregistered if:

"the pupil has ceased to attend the school and the proprietor of the school has received written notification from the parent that the pupil is receiving education otherwise than at school"

Section 434(6) of the same Act also states that:

'A person who contravenes or fails to comply with any requirement imposed on him by regulations under this section is guilty of an offence and liable on summary conviction to a fine not exceeding level 1 on the standard scale.'

Despite our letter [name of head teacher] has refused to deregister our child in accordance with the Act. We are therefore writing to you and ask you to ensure that [child's name] is deregistered from [name of school] immediately.

Yours sincerely,

[Your name]

A head teacher has no power to prevent you from withdrawing your child from their school, no matter how much they might protest and tell you that they do. They have no authority over your decision.

Letter for de-registering a child from a special needs school (in England)

If you have a child that is registered at a special needs school, you will need to write to your Local Authority rather than direct to the school itself.

[Your Address]

[Name of LA Officer]

[LA's address]

[Date]

Dear [Name of the local educational director for your area]

Re: [Name of child. Date of birth. Name of special school attending.]

Our child [name of child] is a registered pupil at [name of school] and we are writing to inform you that we wish to take full responsibility for providing for [name of child]'s education, in accordance with section 7 of the 1996 Education Act, 'otherwise than at school'.

We are therefore writing to ask permission for [child's name] to be deleted from the register in accordance with Regulation 8(2) of the Education (Pupil Registration) Regulations 2006.

We aim to provide [child's name] with an education suitable to his age, ability, and educational needs.

Yours sincerely,

[Your name]

Letter for de-registration from a Welsh school

If your child is registered at a school in Wales, the same rules apply as those in England; under Regulation 9 (1)(c), the name of a pupil has to be deleted immediately from the admissions register.

Parents of children who have been registered at a school in Wales who begin home education must inform the school that they are providing education at home. They do not have to seek permission from the Local Authority in order to do this and the school has an obligation to report the deletion of the name from the register to the Local Authority.

As with English schools, if your child is registered at a special school, you must obtain the permission of the Local Authority as per Regulation 9 (2) of the Education (Pupil Registration) Regulations.

First contact with the Local Authority

You are under no obligation to contact your Local Authority (LA) about your decision to educate your child 'otherwise than at school' unless your child is registered with a special needs school. Many parents who choose to home educate their children are misinformed about this and think that after they have informed their child's school, they then have to also inform the LA. You do not.

When you de-register your child from a school it is the school's responsibility to inform the LA. They have to do this immediately.

We will look at the LA and their role in home education in more depth in Chapter 07, however, the usual case is that as soon as your LA have been notified you will receive a letter from them, usually asking if they can pay you a visit. You will also be sent a questionnaire to fill out for them. **You are under no legal obligation to meet with them, nor are you legally obliged to fill out the questionnaire and return it.** Below is a sample letter that you can copy and send to them, outlining your and your child's rights with regards to any visits from the LA.

[Your Address]

[Name of LA Officer]

[LA's address]

[Date]

Dear [name of LA Officer]

Re: [Name of your child. Date of birth.]

Thank you for your letter and questionnaire regarding [child's name]'s education.

As you know under Section 7 of the Education Act, 1996, I have a responsibility to provide [child's name] with an efficient, full-time education, suitable to his/her age and ability and I feel that it would be in [child's name]'s best interest if his/her education takes place at home.

I realise that the Local Authority has a duty to act if it appears that a parent is not undertaking this responsibility and I also understand that, although I have no legal obligation to respond to any enquiries from the Local Authority, this could be construed as being uncooperative.

I am therefore happy to supply information about [child's name]'s education once we have had enough time to explore home-education, and methods of contact, further. I am under no legal responsibility to agree to any home visits from the Local Authority, but I will keep you informed of [child's name]'s progress via a more convenient method as soon as we have settled into home-education.

Yours sincerely,

[your name]

Top tip

Here are some useful points to remember when de-registering your child.

- Whenever you send a letter concerning your decision to home educate your child to anyone in authority always send it in letter form by post. Don't send an email or a fax – these have a habit of getting lost in cyberspace!
- Ensure that all your child's details are correct on any correspondence you send to anyone.
- Keep a diary to record your contacts – dates of letters sent and dates of replies etc.
- Send any correspondence by recorded delivery so that you have proof of postage.
- Always keep a file/folder with copies of any correspondence you have with schools, LAs or anyone else regarding your child's education.
- You do not have to justify why you are removing your child from school to anyone.
- If you feel it necessary you can include a brief summary of the Law relating to home education as below:

Section 7 of the Education Act 1996 applies to England and Wales:

'The parent of every child of compulsory school age shall cause him to receive efficient full-time education suitable to:

1 His age, ability and aptitude, and
2 Any special educational needs he may have, either by regular attendance at school or otherwise.'

Home education is covered under 'education otherwise'.

Case study: My experience of de-registration

When I de-registered our eldest daughter from school, she was actually between schools. It was the summer holidays and she had just finished primary school and had been allocated a place at the local comprehensive school. I simply wrote to the comprehensive school and told them that we no longer required a place at their school.

When our middle daughter wanted to join her sister and be home schooled, she was in her second year of primary school and I had to go through the de-registration process of writing to the school and informing them that our daughter would not be returning the following term and that I was officially de-registering her.

For me it was a very smooth process and I didn't experience any hostility from her teachers or from her head teacher. In fact, they both applauded me in my efforts to provide an education for our daughters and most people working in the education sector have been very positive in their comments regarding our decision to home educate.

Our youngest daughter has never attended a school, so has never been registered for full-time education anywhere. If your child has never been registered at a school, you are not required to inform anyone of your decision to educate your child from home.

A child who has never been to school

Many parents decide that they wish to home educate their child/children even before they are of school age. Some parents who are travellers do not believe in sending their children to school and will teach them all they need to know themselves. This is one of the reasons why the figures of people that home educate cannot be completely accurate. Although many claim it is in the range of around 50,000, no one can know the exact figure because children who have never been registered at a school cannot possibly be accounted for.

The de-registration process of writing a letter to the head teacher of a school only applies to those children that are already registered at a school, so if you child has never attended a school and you decide that you wish to home educate your child, you do not have to inform the school about your decision.

When your child is five and is due to start infant school, you will receive a letter from the educational department of your local council informing you of the schools local to where you live and encouraging you to apply for a place at one of the schools. You are not obliged to return the forms. Neither do you have to inform the LA of your decision to educate your child from home. You may receive another letter asking where you intend to send your child for an education, again, you do not have to reply to this unless you wish to. If you do reply, you can simply tell them that you intend to educate your child from home.

International countries

For the purpose of the audience of this book the rules and regulations relating to home education are primarily for England, Ireland, Scotland and Wales. If you are looking at home schooling your child in another country it is important to check with the authorities in that country as to whether they allow home education and also how their procedures work.

Case studies: Other experiences of de-registration

'When we decided to withdraw Sam from primary school we were initially told by both his class teacher and the head teacher that it was not in our son's best interests and that although they had no power to stop us, they would be informing the LA of their objections. I was quite upset about this but when I spoke to a home education charity they assured me that neither the school nor the LA could legally do anything about our right to home educate our son.'

Sarah, mother to Sam, eight

'I was terrified of what my daughter's headmistress would say when I nervously posted the letter stating that I wished to de-register Jess from school; I imagined being hauled into the headmistress' office and being given two weeks' detention! In fact, Jess's headmistress was very understanding and told me that school did not suit every child and that every child was unique. She even offered to provide me with a copy of lesson plans for her year should Jess want to continue studying the National Curriculum.'

Marie, mother to Jess, 13

Key points

- No one can be sure just how many children are home educated in the UK, but the figure is estimated to be around 50,000.
- If your child has never been registered at a school, you do not have to inform anyone of your decision to home educate.

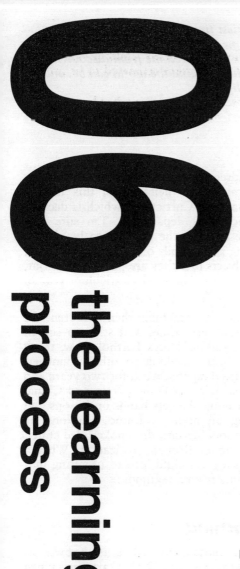

06

the learning process

School was the unhappiest time of my life and the worst trick it ever played on me was to pretend that it was the world in miniature. For it hindered me from discovering how lovely and delightful and kind the world can be, and how much of it is intelligible.

E. M. Forster

Learning styles

As so many different children share classes the school has to limit the subjects they can teach their pupils; this usually consists of teaching the National Curriculum which is decided by the government's educational department. I'm sure that many teachers would love to be in the position to be able to spend quality time teaching their pupils on a one-to-one basis, or teaching their pupils subjects that they are passionate about, instead of having to stick to the National Curriculum year in year out.

Some home educators stick to teaching their children the National Curriculum, follow term times and stick to school hours, others such as the author, James Bartholomew, teach their children by taking them travelling to other countries. James has home schooled his daughter, Alex, for two years and she has enjoyed educational trips to France, Italy and China. Instead of learning from a book she gets hands on lessons and life experience – learning all about volcanic eruptions by climbing up to the rim and looking into the smoke-filled crater, visiting Pompeii to learn about Roman civilization. What a fantastic learning experience for a child instead of sitting in a stuffy classroom and learning from a textbook!

Autonomous learning

My own children learn mostly by what is known as automatic/autonomous learning – that is, they are very much allowed to learn what they want and when they want. They are given the freedom to make choices as to what subjects they would like to study and are under no pressure to study subjects that they show no interest in.

Automatic learning was the phrase coined by American author and educator John Holt in the late 1960s and early 1970s and he has become one of the best-known advocates of home schooling or home education, playing an essential role in making home education an alternative option for parents and their children in the United States.

Holt started his career as a schoolteacher and although successful in his chosen profession, he was also in a position to see the faults in the state-education system in which he was working. He spent his working life studying why children were not learning very much in school and in 1964 he wrote his first best-selling book, *How Children Fail*. In 1967 he earned himself another best-seller in the form of his book, *How Children Learn* which sold over 1.5 million copies.

Whilst teaching at Harvard, Holt continued with his studies into why the schooling system didn't work and by the late 1970s he had come to the conclusion that schools were nothing more than flawed institutions and that parents would be better advised to teach their children at home. As you might expect, he was not popular with his fellow teachers and academics. However, some parents did agree with his viewpoint – parents who wanted to know why their children answered the question of what they had done at school with the standard, bored answer of 'nothing much'.

Unschooling

Holt started up a magazine called *Growing Without Schooling*, in which he set out his extreme philosophy that children who attended school were in nothing more than an institution that they should not be in, and that any form of organized schooling was detrimental to a child's development. Holt's philosophy was as follows:

> 'The human animal is a learning animal; we like to learn; we are good at it; we don't need to be shown how or be made to do it. What kills the processes are the people interfering with it or trying to regulate it or control it.'

In 1980, he later said:

> 'I want to make it clear that I don't see home schooling as some kind of answer to the badness of schools. I think that the home is the proper base for the exploration of the world which we call learning or education. Home would be the best base, no matter how good the schools were. It's not that I feel that school is a good idea gone wrong, but a wrong

idea from the word go. It's a nutty notion that we can have a place where nothing but learning happens, cut off from the rest of life.'

John Holt spent much of the rest of his life campaigning for and supporting home schooling and his studies and findings proved that children learn better when they are not being taught a specific syllabus. Holt termed the learning system as 'unschooling'. The philosophy behind it being that making a group of children all behave the same way and learn in the same way, rather than allowing them to learn at their own pace and through a process of discovery and exploration, was in fact detrimental to their ability to learn effectively.

Although we like to think that home education is new and groundbreaking, there have been other educational writers that have written about alternative ways to educate your child. In 1972, Hal Bennett penned a book entitled *No More Public School*, which explained how to take your child out of public school and educate him/her from home. In 1974, a book called *The 12 Year Sentence*, written and edited by William F. Richenbacker, was a collection of essays proposing that parents should be entitled to teach their own children if they wished to. It was a book written by Ivan Illich called *Deschooling Society*, that was produced in 1971, which was the most influential to John Holt in his quest to bring the subject to a wider audience.

As with anything, Holt had his fair share of critics and some people have said that they feel that a child has to have some form of formal structure in his/her education and that giving them a free rein could lead to a child not learning any important skills that they will need for the future and this debate continues to run. It is worth remembering that a recent study on state-school education showed that in the course of the six hours that a child is at school, they only actually learn anything for one hour a day.

Encouraging autonomous learning

Of course if you have decided to take control of your child's education, you have to take a proactive role in that education, whether it is in the form of formal lessons or baking cakes together all morning. You can no longer drop your kids off at the school gate and let the teachers get on with it. If you left a child unsupervised to simply get on with whatever they wanted to do there is the possibility that they could harm themselves or others by being too inquisitive!

Automatic learning or 'unschooling' will vary from home to home depending on the parents and children alike, the resources available and the interests of the child. You may have a child who is passionate about creating music and will happily spend six hours a day playing and practising the piano. You only have to look at a child playing with their toys to realize that children are very good at managing their own time and do not need to be told to sit down and play, and this applies to their learning. A child who loves to draw will spend all day doing so, just as a child who loves the outdoors will gladly spend hours outside investigating his/her world.

Even before we think of sending our children to school, all their initial learning – how to speak, how to write their own name, how to sing nursery rhymes – is all learnt by us, the parents. It seems only natural to continue with that method of learning. Most parents would hate the idea of another person teaching their child to walk or talk and yet most of us quite happily send them off to allow someone else to take away that natural, parental ability to teach them as soon as they hit five.

Automatic education obviously covers a broad range. Some home-schooling parents do not do any formal or structured lessons with their children at all, whilst others have some formal lessons such as maths and English in a bid to keep them in line with their peers or to establish familiarity to the day so that there is a distinct difference between a 'school' day and a day off.

Many families I have spoken to, and whom are included in this book, have started off with the intention of copying the school system and doing the same formal, structured learning as the schools do, by studying textbooks and allowing them breaks for playtime and lunch etc. However, most have found that this method of learning simply doesn't work for children. They may as well be back in school. As I mentioned in the introduction of this book, I initially spent a small fortune on the appropriate textbooks for my three children and most of them are still in the shopping bag and have never been opened.

Some people have questioned the effectiveness of automatic learning and wonder how on earth a child masters the basic principles of maths, English and other core subjects that we need to know in our society. You will be amazed at how quickly a child will pick up maths skills by playing a game of Monopoly, when they realize that in order to win they need to work out how much money they can make when someone lands on one of their hotels. Weights, measures and home economics can be learned by making fairy cakes and English skills are often learnt by reading cartoon comics, designing and writing their own magazines and even by playing computer games. As James Bartholomew proved, geography skills can be learned much more effectively by actually visiting the country, but if your budget won't stretch to that, then how about creating your very own travel agency where your child can be the boss? Not only will he/she learn about the world, they will also cover business skills, maths and English. History lessons can be covered by exploring your family tree. PE no longer needs to consist of running around a sports field, you can try rock climbing, kayaking, ice skating, swimming, gymnastics, or even dancing around your living room!

The problem we find in this country and many other countries across the world is that many people assume that an education that is provided by the state is the best and only way to educate a child. Unfortunately, because the syllabus is designed so that great numbers of children can be taught a set core of basic subjects, it means that children will only ever experience or have the chance to learn a limited education which is exactly the same as every other child in the country.

The unschooling system covers a wide range of subjects and some parents do not do any formal lessons with their children at all. Children that live in the countryside have more opportunity to explore their surroundings than those that live in a built-up area, but that doesn't mean that a child living in a less stimulating area will suffer. Nowadays, inner cities provide museums, art galleries, zoos and a whole host of free educational activities where a child can gain information.

Many parents presume that if a child is having fun they surely can't be learning anything worth learning. On the contrary, think back to your own schooling days and the lessons and teachers that you preferred going to. There's your answer. The lessons you remembered as most enjoyable are the ones that stick in your mind. Even now, 24 years after leaving school, I still remember everything I learned from my geography lessons because my geography teacher, Mr French, made the subject so enjoyable. It wasn't like having a lesson. He took us out of the classroom to wander around the school field in order to study the effects of weather erosion on different materials and whenever we studied a country he would bring in items from that country, such as silks from India, and make us believe that we were really in that country, despite actually being stuck in a classroom.

A typical day of learning

No two days are the same in our household so I can't really give you a typical day, but this is the type of day that my three children call a 'school' day:

The two younger children will usually wake around 9 a.m. and have a leisurely breakfast for half an hour while they decide what they would like to study. We have found that our eldest daughter, who is a night owl, works best in the evenings and at night. Unless we have planned a day out, 'lessons' generally start around 10 a.m. with both girls doing maths worksheets – these usually consist of basic addition, subtraction, division and multiplication – and sometimes they make up sums for each other. There are many maths and English worksheets available to print free from the Internet. I have found that my children have an attention span of about half an hour before they need to take a break, so by 10.30 a.m. they are done and run off into the garden to the trampoline to play for 20 minutes or so.

When they decide to return we might do some English work. This can range from writing letters to their friends and family, to creating their own magazines, learning punctuation or grammar or writing a review for a book. I'm not in any way strict about setting lesson plans; if they want to write a letter to a friend, I know that as we write it they are learning how to punctuate and write a grammatically correct piece of work. I do not stand over them because I feel that if they need my help they will ask for it, so I am often at my desk working.

After another 30 minutes we might decide to go to the shops and buy something for our lunch. I often allow the children to do the shopping and this will include working out how much things will cost and how much change we will have left over (maths). As I work in journalism and publishing I tend to buy a selection of daily newspapers, so during lunchtime we might discuss something that has been in the news recently. This often leads to heated debates which will continue throughout the day and often spark an idea for a project. For example, there was recently an article in the press about whether fashion designers should use bigger sized models to represent the average sized woman. This led to my eldest daughter writing an essay on the size zero issue and how it can be associated with anorexia. More recently we have been discussing the effects of a recession, which has led our older two girls to enter a writing competition to write a story on the theme. The prize is £100 – a good incentive!

After lunch we might go swimming or ice skating, but often the children will do their own thing. There is a lot of argument that children will get lazy if left to their own devices and do nothing but watch TV. Children soon get bored with doing nothing at all and even the most devoted TV addict will get fed up with watching cartoons all day. Children are naturally inquisitive and a simple question such as 'Why is the sky blue?' will set their imagination alight and they will want to investigate and find out the answers to their own question.

Sometimes we will do some baking in the afternoon, which will lead to learning about weights and measures; other times the children might decide to create a shop, a bakery or a bank. It's a bit of a free-for-all during the afternoons and as long as they have done some written and maths work during the morning, I generally allow them to do their own thing in the afternoons. Some weeks it might be playing computer games, others it might be trying to recreate a painting of the Mona Lisa. Our middle daughter is passionate about animals, so we might visit the zoo or she might work on a project about a particular animal in the afternoon.

Our history lessons have consisted of formulating our family tree, visiting places of interest and watching documentaries together. Geography lessons have been to pick a country from a map of the world and create a project about it. We do not have a great deal of disposable income, so we need to be imaginative in the things that we do for 'lessons', but this isn't too difficult as children are great at using their imaginations!

All the children are interested in photography and as I studied the subject at City and Guilds level I often set them assignments of subjects that they need to photograph. This often turns into a healthy competition of who can get the best shot and our eldest daughter is brilliant at manipulating her images using Photoshop. The younger two often pretend that they are on an undercover assignment and have to get their shots without anyone seeing them!

The children all have fantastic computer skills and have even created their own websites. Whenever they have a question that needs answering they will often research pages on the Internet and find the answer for themselves.

A theatre visit to see Andrew Lloyd Webber's *Cats* led our 12-year-old daughter to study the complete works of poet T. S. Elliot and in particular his *Old Possum's Book of Practical Cats* on which the production was based.

When we decided to replace our kitchen cupboards one year, we didn't bother hiring someone in to do it, we worked it out together and between us all we managed to re-face the kitchen.

The way in which we educate our children is not only more relaxing for them it is also great fun. Recently we started a project about World War II and they made ration books and pretended that they were evacuees. Another discussion about recycling led to my middle daughter and my husband creating their own vegetable plot and compost bin at the back of the garden. This year they have grown sweetcorn, potatoes, runner beans, cabbages, beetroot, parsnips, tomatoes, onions and broccoli and our daughter has learned what can and can't be recycled.

We don't tend to stick to the standard school times of 9 a.m. to 3 p.m. because we find this to be too constricting, especially if we are out for the day. However, I do follow the same term times as the schools and allow them to have the same holidays as their school friends because this gives them an opportunity to catch up with other children. Whilst some may argue that we don't have a completely autonomous style of learning, because I do think it is important to encourage a child to read and write, their day-to-day learning is very non-structured and very much up to them.

Top tip

PE doesn't have to mean running on the spot in a sweaty gym! You can keep your children fit by taking all sorts of sports classes, working out to a fitness DVD or jumping on the trampoline for half an hour a day – the latter is great fun even for an adult!

Case Studies: Variations of a typical day of home education

'Having discovered that at the age of seven our daughter still couldn't read properly and could barely write her own name and address or add up, we wondered quite what the school we had sent her to was actually teaching her. After all, surely the most important thing children should be taught is to read and write properly? We had heard about how popular home education or home schooling was in America from some of our friends who lived over there and decided that it would be a better option for our daughter, if only for a few years to enable her to be able to spend the majority of the time actually learning to read properly.

At first I believed that I had to separate school things from fun things and started our daughter's home education full of enthusiasm with timetables, lists, lots and lots of appropriate reading materials and textbooks. We would do half-hour slots of reading, writing and maths and this lasted for all of two days. My daughter's attention span was not great and she complained that it was boring just adding up numbers, so I took her to the supermarket, handed her a list of groceries that she needed to buy and gave her my purse. She skipped around the shop, checking the prices on the items and to my surprise she even bought the lower priced items in a bid to save me some money. When she got to the checkout the lady behind the till asked her why she wasn't at school and she proudly announced that she was home educated.

Although I felt guilty that we were going to fun and interesting places like the local museum, playing in the park and taking the first train that came along and seeing where it took us, rather than sitting down at a desk and ploughing through a Key Stage book, I could tell that she was absorbing much more information and at a faster rate than she had ever done at school. Within three months my daughter was reading books designed for 12 year olds and, more importantly, was reading them because she wanted to read them and not because I had told her to.

This was nine years ago and we now have three other children aged between three and 12. All our children are being home educated and I have discovered that having a fixed structure simply doesn't work for us. It doesn't suit our children who love to find things out for themselves – which is a good job really because I didn't relish the idea of having to re-learn fractions in order to teach them! It is almost impossible for me to teach multiplication to one child, whilst teaching another to read, explaining what the stock market is to the eldest and baking fairy cakes with the two year old, so we don't bother with any form of structure these days!

Most days the children will do some written and mathematic work and this might just be making up lyrics to a song or counting the apples on the tree in the nearby orchard. The children have very different interests but they all play together, draw, read, write, play instruments and help each other, and all without me telling them. In fact, it is easier than when our daughter was at school!

We all watch documentaries together and have what we call a 'kitchen science' day where we will drag the ancient chemistry set out and make papier-mâché volcanoes using bicarbonate of soda and lots of red food colouring to create the lava. Our PE lessons usually consist of swimming at the local pool or going for long nature walks. Whenever the kids want to do craftwork, depending on the weather, we will take the paints, clay, and other materials into the garden and spend the day creating collages or painting family portraits of each other in the style of a famous artist.

Having children who love to learn and who are always busy making, doing and discovering has made education easy and enjoyable for them and me. We learn about different cultures by hearing about it on the news and then deciding to do a project on it. We once paid a visit to a real Romany gypsy who had camped up in a field near to our house. He had a traditional horse-drawn gypsy caravan and happily told the children all about his culture and the true Romany ways. This led our eldest daughter to write a project about travellers which she used instead of formal examination results to gain entry into college last year.

My role as a 'teacher' is more about listening to what the children have found out themselves, rather than teaching them anything specific. I obviously help them if they have a question and if I can't answer it, we will find someone who can. We are always being told by the government to get back to basics and yet they still insist that an education is when children are crammed into a classroom and taught boring subjects to memorize in order to pass an exam just because that is what everyone else is doing.

My children have had the opportunity to learn things that they would never have been able to learn at school. Our eldest son, who is 12, is passionate about modern music and has been able to spend the past three months in a recording studio seeing how music is produced and all because he wrote to a recording studio and asked if he could have some work experience to see whether he would like to pursue this career in the future. I don't know of anyone who says that they loved going to school as a child, but my children jump out of bed excited at the prospect of what the day holds for them. They and I had no idea education could be this much fun.

Of course, we have some off-days too, where it's pouring with rain outside and we are all driving each other mad, but then tell me what family doesn't? I occasionally long for a bath without being invaded with questions such as 'How is water filtered so that we can drink it?' And when someone has put too much bicarbonate of soda into the volcano and I have red blotches all over the kitchen walls sometimes I do question my decision to home educate! But on the whole, we feel that our life is perfect and couldn't get any better!'

Jane, home-educating parent to Amanda, Noah, James and Freddie

'I never really liked school. I hated getting up really early in the mornings, I hated the long walk to school and I didn't much like the teachers either. Because I'm quite small, I was teased a lot at school and I didn't like that. I would never tease someone because of their height, but people seemed to think it was OK to tease me. One day a boy in my class took my lunchbox and threw it into the stream that ran alongside the school. I told my teacher and she just said that I would have to pay for a school dinner instead. She didn't even tell the boy off.

When my dad came to pick me up he was really cross about what had happened and told the teacher off and said I wouldn't be coming back to school again. I didn't know that children could be educated at home, but my mum and dad did. I wish I had known before because I wouldn't have gone in the first place.

I could already read and write so my mum and dad said that it was up to me what I wanted to do at home, which was really cool. I've always loved sports, especially cricket and I want to play for England one day. I thought there was no way that my mum and dad would allow me to just do sports all day long, but guess what? They did! They said as long as I continued to read books and do some maths worksheets every day, the rest of the time I could go to the local leisure centre and play as much sport as I wanted.

At first I had to stick to things like swimming and running during the week because everyone else was at school, but then my mum found a group of other home educators. We played rounders, went ice skating and even started our own sports club because one of the other children's parents used to be a PE teacher.

I've been educated at home now for two years and I love it. I don't see why I should have to put up with being teased and bullied just because of my height and I don't see why teachers should be allowed to just let bullying happen. When my little sister saw that I was having so much fun, she also wanted to be home educated, so now neither of us go to school, which is good because it gives me someone to play football with, although she's not that good at it. I still have lots of friends that I play with from school, but I also have lots of friends who are home educated, so I have the best of both worlds.

I don't ever want to go back to school. I play for my local cricket team and I do everything that I love. When I'm older, I'm going to play for the England team.'

Noah, aged 12, educated from home for two years

National Curriculum learning

Many parents, when starting out in home education, automatically start by keeping to the same curriculum as the schools because this is how their children have been used to learning and they want to instill the same structure at home as was in the school. This is not my preferred way of learning because I feel that the whole purpose of leaving the state system for us as a family was to give our children a better and more fulfilling education than any school could provide.

However, many parents feel happier following the National Curriculum and some even prefer to follow the school style of learning – having a separate room as a classroom complete with desks and a whiteboard and even ringing a bell at 9 a.m. to signal the beginning of lessons.

If you are going to follow a curriculum learning method, you will need to buy all the relevant materials for each lesson and those relevant to your child's age. The National Curriculum is a series of set subjects that all state-school children will learn from the age of five until they are 16. Every child that attends a state school will be taught exactly the same syllabus which is decided by our government's educational department.

Unfortunately there is no government funding for children that are home educated so if you are going to teach your child in accordance with the National Curriculum you are going to have to buy the necessary books and materials in line with the ones that they use in schools. This is perfectly doable, although there can be problems when it comes to subjects such as chemistry and physics. Many home-educating parents have found the solution to this is to group together and hire a science lab for scientific subjects.

The National Curriculum sets out the stages and core subjects that your child will be taught during their time at school. Although free to plan and organize lessons and teaching techniques, every state-funded school must teach the National Curriculum. It was designed to ensure that all state schools learn the same subjects and at the same levels.

The National Curriculum sets out:

- the subjects taught
- the skills and understanding required for each subject
- targets that a child is expected to meet in relation to every other child of the same age
- how children are assessed and tested.

Key stages

Many schools use the Qualifications and Curriculum Authority (QCA) Schemes of Work to plan their curriculum. These help to translate the National Curriculum's objectives into teaching and learning activities. The National Curriculum is organized into set blocks of years, known as Key Stages. If you are going to teach your child in accordance with the National Curriculum, you will need to be aware of the Key Stages and the appropriate learning materials and lessons as below. There are four Key Stages plus one Foundation Stage:

Age	Stage	Year
3–4	Foundation	Pre-school
4–5	Foundation	Reception
5–6	Key Stage 1	Year 1
6–7	Key Stage 1	Year 2
7–8	Key Stage 2	Year 3
8–9	Key Stage 2	Year 4
9–10	Key Stage 2	Year 5
10–11	Key Stage 2	Year 6
11–12	Key Stage 3	Year 7
12–13	Key Stage 3	Year 8
13–14	Key Stage 3	Year 9
14–15	Key Stage 4	Year 10
15–16	Key Stage 4	Year 11

Each subject in the National Curriculum has its own study programme and many parents prefer this method of teaching because it sets out exactly what other children that go to school are learning. This way you can be assured that your child is learning in the same way as schoolchildren are. It can also be an easy way to assess whether your child is working at the same level as every other child his/her age.

In nearly all the National Curriculum subjects there is a scale of attainment within that subject. These are known as targets and are split into eight levels. The exception is Citizenship, which has separate attainment targets for the end of Key Stages 3 and 4. Because children develop at different rates, it is thought that by setting attainment targets you will get an idea of how your child is progressing compared to what is thought to be typical for other children of the same age. This method of learning has been very much debated over the years because whilst some children excel in one subject another child might not enjoy that particular subject and excel in something completely different, such as sports.

In school, your child's teacher will carry out regular checks on their progress in each subject. At the end of Key Stages 1, 2 and 3 they will carry out a formal teaching assessment which will highlight which subjects your child excels in and which he/she doesn't. At Key Stages 2 and 3, your child, if at school, will be tested in accordance with the national tests for every other school child and this will be in English and maths. There are also tests to determine which GCSEs your child will do well in. There is nothing to stop your child from studying the National Curriculum from home and taking GCSEs as an external student. We will discuss this more in Chapter 09.

The reason why many parents choose to teach their children at home is because of the National Curriculum, its limited subjects and the constant testing and meeting target requirements. I know many teachers that would prefer to be able to teach their children more diverse subjects than what are on offer in the National Curriculum.

Compulsory subjects

Key Stage 1 and 2

Compulsory National Curriculum subjects for Key Stages 1 and 2 are as follows:

- English
- Maths
- Science
- Design and technology
- Information and communication technology (ICT)
- History
- Geography
- Art and design
- Music
- Physical education
- At least one foreign language.

Schools also have to teach religious education, though parents have the right to withdraw children for all or part of the religious education curriculum. In addition, schools are advised to teach personal, social and health education (PSHE) and citizenship. Schools may cover these subjects under different names, and may teach more than one subject together under the same name. This is left up to individual schools, but they are a compulsory part of the National Curriculum.

Key Stage 3

Children attending a state school from age 11–14 (Years 7–9) follow Key Stage 3 of the National Curriculum. The subjects for this Key Stage are:

- English
- Maths
- Science
- Design and technology
- Information and communication technology (ICT)
- History
- Geography
- Modern foreign languages
- Art and design
- Music
- Citizenship
- Physical education.

Schools also have to provide:

- Careers education and guidance (during Year 9)
- Sex and relationship education (SRE)
- Religious education.

Depending on the school, your child may also have lessons in personal, social and health education (PSHE).

Key Stage 4

If your child was at school at the age of 14 he/she would take national tests in English, maths and science. During Year 9 your child would also choose the subjects that they wish to study for Key Stage 4. Many of these subjects will lead to the GCSEs that they would take.

School children aged between 14 and 16 usually work towards their chosen GCSEs. In Key Stage 4 there are also six compulsory subjects:

- English
- Maths
- Science
- Information and communication technology (ICT)
- Physical education
- Citizenship.

Changes in the National Curriculum

The National Curriculum has come under a lot of criticism in recent years. In September 2007 a new secondary curriculum was published, intended to give schools more flexibility. The new curriculum aims to:

- cut back on the amount of compulsory subject content
- give teachers more time and space to personalize their teaching by offering catch-up lessons in the basics, and creating opportunities for all pupils to deepen and extend their learning
- develop a stronger focus on the development of personal attributes and practical life skills
- help teachers to make connections between the subjects and to view the curriculum as a whole.

The new Key Stage 3 curriculum will be brought in over a three-year period. It became compulsory for Year 7 pupils in September 2008. From September 2009, it will apply to all Year 7 and Year 8 pupils, and from September 2010 it will apply across Years 7, 8 and 9. Changes to the Key Stage 4 curriculum will be brought in from September 2009. It is worth bearing in mind that if you are going to teach your child the National Curriculum, you will need to be aware of any changes that the government make.

Another recent change that has been brought into force is the introduction of working towards Diplomas instead of GCSEs. In September 2008, the New Diploma qualification was introduced alongside GCSEs and A Levels in selected schools and colleges. The government has suggested that the New Diploma could replace GCSEs and A Levels for all 14–19 year olds. It is thought that GCSEs and A Levels will still be on offer until at least 2015.

The New Diploma is a new qualification designed for 14–19 year olds which offers a more practical way of gaining a recognized qualification and one that employers and universities will accept instead of academic qualifications. Currently there are five subjects available in selected schools and colleges. These are:

- Construction and the built environment
- Creative and media
- Engineering
- Information technology
- Society, health and development.

As a home educator it can be difficult to cover the New Diploma syllabus due to the amount of hands on experience required outside of the classroom, but many local colleges will now take home-educated children if they are interested in gaining a Diploma.

Case study: Teaching the National Curriculum from home

'When we decided to home educate our two children, Jack, eight, and Tia, ten, they had both been going to the local school. Tia was due to go to the nearest comprehensive, but because we lived just outside of the catchment area it meant that she wasn't entitled to a free bus pass so we were told that we would have to pay for her place on the coach. This worked out at almost £400 per year. Jack had been having problems with bullying in school and we later discovered that he was dyslexic and simply couldn't keep up with the pace of the lessons at school.

Because they had already been used to the structure at school and I used to be a primary teacher, we decided that we would continue this and use the dining room as our schoolroom. We put three desks in there, covered the walls in educational posters and we even invested in a Bunsun burner for when we did science lessons. The children loved this because it separated their school time from their playing time and they knew that once we shut the door to the dining room, school was over for the day.

I decided to continue with the National Curriculum because this is what the children were used to and also because it would make things a whole lot easier for me if I could set them work from an already-established study plan. Jack and Tia found it easier too because they knew that they were working in line with other children their own age.

It has cost us considerably more to teach the children the same way as schools because we have had to buy all the relevant learning materials and textbooks. I got a full study plan for both the children's relevant years from the Department of Education.

Our school day starts at 9 a.m. and we have a 30-minute break at 11 a.m. We will then work until 1 p.m. and break for lunch. In the afternoons we will do some vocational learning or sports and will finish at 3.30 p.m., the same as the children's friends that go to school.

Tia has just begun working towards her GCSEs and we will have to pay for each exam and enter her as an external student, but I feel that it's a small price to pay for exams that are recognized by colleges. Jack decided a year ago that he no longer wanted to follow the National Curriculum but wanted to learn about engineering, so although we continue to study some of the core subjects, he has dropped some subjects like art and IT in favour of studying engineering and physics.

There is no difference to the children's learning other than them being in their own environment and of course having one-to-one tuition.'

Lizzy, home educator to Tia, 14, and Jack, 11

Top tip

Ask your children what they want to learn about – they will certainly let you know!

Montessori learning

An Italian doctor by the name of Maria Montessori was responsible for the Montessori method of learning. Maria Montessori was the first woman in Italy to qualify as a physician and she developed an interest in the diseases of children and in particular those that were said to be uneducable. Having spent a number of years studying the behaviour of children and the way they learnt, she developed a programme of training for teachers, drawing on educators Froebelian and Rousseau's theories that children learn better through play. Montessori's programme enabled children that had been written off as stupid to learn to read and write. Her teaching method was different to how schools taught children in that instead of learning by repetition, children would learn by doing and being naturally inquisitive. So, looking would become reading and touching would become writing.

The success of her method caused her to question the normal education that children were receiving and in which many children were failing. Maria Montessori decided to test her theories on a wider scale by opening the first Montessori school in Rome in 1907.

The house where she set up her first school was designed to provide a good environment for children to live and learn and the emphasis was on self-development, rather than being told what to do. The 'teacher' of a Montessori school is the 'keeper' or 'over-seer' of the school rather than someone that has the last word. This enables everyone to be equal from the start. The job of the 'keeper' is to simply observe activities and ensure that the children are safe.

The Montessori schooling system is one that incorporates 'classes' of children of all ages and abilities and is very much a child-led programme. Older children will help the younger children and class sizes are usually no more than 20. Many Montessori schools cater only for children from the ages of two to five, but there are a few that extend that age range to 16.

Today there are more than 5,000 Montessori schools in the US and around 600 in the UK, all of which are privately funded. The Montessori method is one that many home educators choose for their children because it is a highly hands-on approach to learning and encourages children to think for themselves, ask questions and work things out for themselves by doing many different activities.

Montessori classrooms are designed to provide an atmosphere that is a natural and peaceful environment and this is one of the reasons why many home-educating parents choose this method of learning for their children. Nothing is out of bounds in a Montessori classroom and children have access to both the classroom and the outdoors, providing as much access to everything in their world as possible.

The core areas

There are six overall areas in the Montessori Curriculum:

Practical life
This area is designed to help students develop and care for themselves, the environment and each other. In the Primary years, aged between three and six, children learn how to do things such as pouring and scooping using various kitchen utensils, washing dishes, shining objects, scrubbing tables and cleaning up.

Children also learn how to dress themselves, tie their shoelaces, wash their hands and other various self-care needs. They learn these through a wide variety of materials and activities. They learn what can and can't be recycled and how important it is, for the future of our planet, to care for the environment.

Sensorial

All our learning first comes to us through the senses. The Montessori method has shown that by isolating something that is being taught the child can focus more easily on it. So, for example, learning colours by associating coloured items is difficult for children to grasp. In the Montessori method colours are taught with colour tablets. The colour tablets are all exactly the same except for one thing – the colour in the middle. This helps take away the confusion for the child and helps them to focus on specifically what a colour is.

Cultural

Children taught under the Montessori method learn about the world around them and study different cultures. From a very early age they are taught about different countries around the world, different environments and different religions. The Montessori method uses coloured maps in order to help children remember continents, countries and states, and to get an understanding of the different cultures in the world. More importantly, the goal is to get an understanding that there are various cultures and these cultures have a lot to offer us.

Science

It has been found that Montessori children have excellent detail skills. This is due to the fact that there are no limits placed upon what they can and can't study and nothing is taboo. From an early age children are encouraged to find things out for themselves and this is particularly so in the subject of science. Science lessons are all about finding out how things work. For example, a study of a particular animal will include wanting to know all the various body parts and what part they play in that animal's life. They will discover the life cycles of different animals and study the animal in depth until they run out of questions and have satisfied themselves that they know everything they wish to know about it.

Language

The language curriculum in a Montessori school involves everything from vocabulary development to writing and then to reading. Children learn their basic letter sounds through the use of sandpaper letters, where the letters are cut from sandpaper and glued to a wooden board. As the child traces the letter, they get a real feel for how the letter flows. They can also feel if a mistake is made because of the different feel of the sandpaper from the board. They begin making words before they can read words with the moveable alphabet, a large box of cut out letters made from wood that the child can arrange on his or her rug.

Children learn about nouns, verbs, adjectives, articles, prepositions, adverbs, conjunctions, pronouns and interjections all by examples, rather than by textbook. This means that they learn how to write and speak correctly from the beginning rather than picking up bad habits and having to re-learn the correct way.

Maths

A Montessori maths lesson is a very hands-on and practical lesson which enables the child to remember and work things out for themselves by doing, rather than by being taught on a whiteboard. Children learn the difference between units of tens by using practical materials such as maths towers. They also use the Montessori Bead, which is an extension of the abacus system.

Because children are aware of their senses at a very early age, every 'lesson' incorporates a sensorial-based learning system. This method is particularly effective for children that may be dyslexic and who learn better by doing and working things out for themselves in a practical way rather than being told what to do.

Every activity has its place in a Montessori classroom and although it may look simple and like a playgroup, there is a reason why everything is how it is. It is because studies have shown that children learn better by doing and investigating for themselves than by being told to sit down and face the front of the class.

Many home educators find that both the philosophy and the materials that the Montessori method use are very useful because each child is treated as an individual and the activities are designed to be ones of self-learning and self-discovery.

Many aspects of the Montessori method can be scaled down to a home-schooling environment such as making lessons look like play rather than work – cleaning up after themselves, taking responsibility for their actions, accepting people and finding out about other people's cultures, religions and politics.

Montessori method and exams

The Montessori method focuses on personal development rather than tests and exams and has been shown to produce more mature, creative and socially adept children. A study in the US carried out by psychologists on children being taught by the Montessori method showed that they out-performed children given a traditional education. Children who have been taught the Montessori way are better equipped at maths and writing from an early age and can easily participate in exams and tests.

The current GCSEs and A Level exams, that are standard practice within state-funded schools, are basically based around the practice of reading and remembering the relevant syllabus for each GCSE subject. Unfortunately, we are still in a culture where because the majority of children attend a state education, the majority of schools, colleges and employers only recognize a child's ability in relation to how many state exams they have taken and what grade they achieved.

Regardless of how you decide to home educate your child, you can still enter your child into qualifications that are recognized by employers and colleges. Just as you or I as an adult would be able to study a GCSE or A Level subject and then enter ourselves for the exam, so too can any child, regardless of whether they have studied that subject before or not. We will look at taking exams as an external student in Chapter 09. It is worth remembering that many schools are now opting out of the National Curriculum in favour of more practical, hands-on learning methods, such as the Montessori method.

The National Curriculum was designed to give all children attending state schools the same basic education across the board and all state-funded schools are required by law to follow this system of learning and to adhere to national testing and exams. As mentioned before, there has been a lot of criticism about the National Curriculum from parents, pupils and even teachers. Although state-funded education is free to anyone that wants it, it also comes at a price – your child *has* to learn whatever is on the National Curriculum.

However, there is a loophole within the 1988 Education Act that has recently come to light. Hidden deep in the government's legislation for education is an opt-out clause. This lies in the National Curriculum. The National Curriculum is the national examination syllabus, which is what all the GCSEs and A Levels are based on. Without that syllabus there can be no SATS or league tables.

Section 16 of the 1988 Education Reform Act states that:

> 'For the purpose of enabling development work or experiments to be carried out, the Secretary of State may direct as respects a particular maintained school that, for such period as may be specified in the direction, the provisions of the National Curriculum –
>
> **a** Shall not apply; or
> **b** Shall apply with such modifications as may be so specified.'

In layman's terms this means that with the Secretary of State's permission, any school may opt out of teaching the National Curriculum in part or whole. The school would have to convince the Secretary of State that it was working towards bettering education for their pupils and prove that a new way of learning is a better way of learning than that of the National Curriculum. To date several state-funded schools are investigating this, so in the future the whole National Curriculum could be a thing of the past.

Case study: Home education and Montessori

'I had heard about the Montessori method of learning years ago when I lived in the States. There are many Montessori teachers practising there and I decided that this was the most natural way for a child to learn – by doing, rather than by being told what to do.

When I had my own children I decided right from the start that they would have a Montessori education, however, at the time there were very few Montessori schools in the UK and none near to where we lived. It was then that my husband suggested that I train as a Montessori teacher and teach the children myself. I had heard about home schooling before, again when I was in America, and thought this might just be the answer.

I trained with the Montessori Centre International as a distance learner because our children were only two and three at the time. It wasn't cheap, but I did manage to get some financial help from the government.

Within 18 months I was a fully trained Montessori teacher and during my training, I put into practice what I learned by teaching my children the Montessori way. Three years on and we have our own little Montessori schooling system. Instead of pretending to cook, the children actually learn to cook; instead of sitting down with a maths worksheet, the children will work calculations out by practical methods such as using wooden sticks and dividing them up into equal numbers for division, or adding them together for addition. The system makes it look as though there is no structure to their learning, but that's the clever thing about it; the way it has been designed makes children think that they are not at school doing boring lessons, but having hours of fun, simply doing what they want.

Some days we will spend hours on long nature walks, making nature trails and identifying the many different species of trees, fungi or animals. Other days, when the weather is not so good, we will cook, paint, build tents in the living room and 'camp out' for the afternoon. No two days are the same. I don't believe that children should be tested for their ability to do something and then compared to the national average, so there are no tests. I monitor what they do and I write lots of notes, but they soon tell me if they don't understand something!

I plan to open my own Montessori school in a few years' time and although many in the UK only cater for the early years, I intend to open a school for children of all ages and abilities.'

Anna, Montessori teacher and home educator to Lilly, five and Anton, six

Internet schooling

Internet schooling is a new concept in learning and many home educators have signed their children up to this style of learning in a bid to ensure that they are kept up to date with the same lessons as their school-attending peers.

The curriculum of Internet schooling is based on the same principles as the National Curriculum and for most Internet schools the subjects a child can study are:

- English
- Maths
- History
- Geography
- Combined Science
- French
- Philosophy

- Art and web design
- Spanish
- German.

The system of Internet schooling is ideal for a child that has suffered bullying or simply does not like a classroom environment, but enjoys a structured way of learning and wishes to study the subjects that are taught in a normal school.

At a cost of around £600 per term, plus equipment such as an up-to-date computer, a good Internet connection and curriculum books etc., it is not as cheap as autonomous learning. However, it is good value when you consider that your child is getting a qualified virtual teacher and will be studying the same as he/she would in a traditional school environment.

'School' starts at 9 a.m. when your child will log on to the Internet and will be able to chat virtually to other classmates in a safe chat area. At 9.30 a.m. classes start and your child's virtual teacher will begin lessons. A timetable will have already been established and all children of the same age will participate by asking and answering questions to the teacher and have class discussions. There is then a break at around 10.30 a.m. and the second lesson of the day will begin at 11 a.m. Lunch is from 12 noon to 1 p.m. and then classes continue until 2 p.m., when everyone will log off for the day.

Internet schooling is ideal for children aged 12 and upwards because they are usually already used to working with modern technology and adapt to this method of learning very well. The other obvious appealing reasons why children enjoy learning virtually include no school uniform, shorter work days, shorter school weeks, and if you have a problem or don't understand something your virtual teacher can help there and then, so no waiting around with your hand in the air.

As with most new things, Internet schooling has also come under criticism from people who say that it is an unhealthy and unsociable alternative to schooling because a child is not physically interacting with other people – only with names on a computer screen. To combat this, some Internet schools have introduced webcams and microphones so that there is more individual participation in class and parents argue that their children are just as active as other children because they still go out to play after school and do physical activities during the weekend.

One Internet school, InterHigh, founded in 2005, is modelled on a typical English/Welsh secondary or comprehensive school and provides virtual schooling for children aged between 11 and 17. Teachers and pupils work from home by logging into a virtual classroom on the Internet to receive real-time tuition every weekday morning. Apart from lessons, teachers set and mark homework, prepare reports, mark end of year exams and prepare pupils for the GCSEs and A levels of their choice in their final year.

All the lessons are taught by experienced, professional teachers and the teachers try to make the lessons as fun as possible. InterHigh have eight qualified teachers on board at present and they only take a maximum of 30 pupils in any one school year. Teaching methods vary with each Internet school: InterHigh, for example, have virtual, real-time class lessons during the mornings, then children are able to organize their own work for the afternoon, although the teachers do set homework and expect it to be returned. The school believes in developing individual responsibility among the students to take control of their lives and achieve their goals. Students monitor their own progress and use self-assessment techniques to chart their progress.

Case study: Cyber school

'I never liked school and disliked it even more when I had to move up to the local comprehensive school and become one of 3,000 pupils. I didn't mind the work; in fact that was the bit I really enjoyed – the lessons. What I didn't like was the fact that every lesson was constantly interrupted by someone that didn't want to learn anything. They would start a fight at the back of the class, or just disrupt the class until the teacher had to stop teaching and sort them out. I didn't feel as though I was learning anything of any importance at school and if I had a question I might have just as well found out the answer myself because the teacher just wanted to get on with the lesson and go home.

A friend of my dad's told us about Internet schooling and I asked my parents if we could look into it as I felt that my time was being wasted at school. I still wanted to study the National Curriculum, but I was getting sick and tired of every lesson being interrupted and not really learning anything and having to teach myself with my textbooks at home after school instead. What's the point in that?

My mum was initially worried that I wouldn't have any friends if I just spent all day learning on the computer, but I've still got loads of friends from school that I hang about with at the weekends or after school.

My lessons start at 9.15 a.m. and each student has to log on. We have a lesson plan relevant to our ages, so if for example I have a maths lesson, my mate Alex, who is a year younger than me, might have an English lesson at the same time, but with different teachers and in different classes. After a half-hour lesson, we stop for a 15-minute break and then continue with whatever subject we were studying for another half hour. We break again for 15 minutes and then go on to another subject until midday, when we break for lunch.

A lot of us tend to spend lunchtime in the 'common room' – an Internet chat room – and we will eat our lunch at our desks and chat about normal teenager things. From 1.30 p.m. until 2.30 p.m. we work on individual projects such as IT skills or web-designing and then we finish our school day at 2.45 p.m.

It's much better than school because we get to get on with our work without any interruptions, and if we have a question the teacher is just a click away. I hope to be able to continue to learn this way, take my GCSEs and then go to college to study web development.'

Stewart, 14, Internet pupil

Flexi-time schooling

Flexi-time schooling is another option that is open to parents who wish to educate their children from home, but who also feel that they need the security of a more structured-based learning that a school can offer.

Flexi-time schooling is often suggested if a child has been having problems adapting to full-time schooling, has experienced bullying or cannot keep up with the demands of a traditional school. Many parents are requesting a more flexible approach to school and all head teachers have the authority to agree to flexi-schooling, although not many make this public knowledge. A flexi-schooling system is, as the name suggests, an arrangement between the parents and the school where their child will spend some of the school week at school and other parts being educated at home by their parents. This is arranged by the head teacher rather than by the Local Authority. The child will still be registered as a pupil with a school but will only attend that school part time.

In England, flexi-schooling is governed by the Education (Pupil Registration) Regulations 2006. Regulation 6 (1) (a) (iii) states that schools must indicate on their register the days that flexi-schooled children are educated at home. Under Regulation 6 (4), the time that a child is being taught at home must be with an approved person and must be of an educational nature – although this does not necessarily have to be the National Curriculum. The school is required to mark the register with Code B, which means educated off-site, rather than Code C, which stands for authorized absence, which counts towards the school's total absence scores.

Flexi-schooling in Wales and Scotland

Flexi-schooling in Wales is also legal and is covered under the Education (Pupil Registration) Regulations 1995. Regulation 7 (1a) states that the school must state on the register when a child is in an out-of-school educational activity.

In Scotland, flexi-schooling regulations are similar to those of England and Wales and parents have to get permission from the head teacher for flexi-schooling.

Considerations when flexi-schooling

It pays to remember that children that are flexi-schooled are still registered pupils of the school and are the responsibility of that school and will have to adhere to the school's rules and regulations when in school hours. They are also required to take the National Curriculum tests such as SATS. In this case flexi-schooling might affect your child's learning in a negative way. If he/she is only attending school part-time, for example, three days a week, there are going to be lessons or parts of lessons that he/she is going to miss. This can make it difficult for a child to keep up with lessons and may have a detrimental effect on the tests they will be expected to take. If, however, home schooling is being followed in accordance with the class lessons during the time when a child is being taught at home, then this should not present a problem.

Because schools are very concerned about attendance figures, many head teachers won't consider flexi-schooling. Any school can accommodate flexi-schooling if it wishes to, but no school is under any obligation to do so. This is where either full-time home education or full-time school prevails, where either the parents choose to completely withdraw their child from school or the Local Authority have to provide a school place for a child. In the case of flexi-schooling, a school does not have to accept a pupil that wishes to go to school part-time and even if they do, parents are still bound by the school rules, even though their child might only go to school a couple of days a week. If a child is flexi-schooled they will get all or part of their education funded.

Flexi-schooling is not something that a parent can demand and you need to have a good, strong case to present to the head teacher, otherwise the school would have children coming and going all over the place. If, for example, your child is a child actor and often needs time off for filming, a head teacher would probably be quite happy for your child to be flexi-schooled to enable him/her to attend auditions and/or filming. The same applies if your child is a child model – although in both cases you have to apply for a special licence from your local council if your child works in the entertainment industry.

In November 2007 the Department for Children, Schools and Families (DCSF) published new guidelines for Local Authorities in relation to flexi schooling. It states that:

> 'Flexi-schooling' or 'flexible school attendance' is an arrangement between the parent and the school where the child is registered at school and attends the school only part time; the rest of the time the child is home educated (on authorized absence from school). This can be a long-term arrangement or a short-term measure for a particular reason. 'Flexi-schooling' is a legal option provided that the head teacher at the school concerned agrees to the arrangement. The child will be required to follow the National Curriculum whilst at school but not whilst he or she is being educated at home. Local authorities should make sure that head teachers are made familiar with flexi-schooling and how it may work in practice.'

The guidelines also set out what they feel is suitable off-site education and what a school can approve. If a school believes that an out-of-school activity is not of an educational nature then they can insist that the child is returned to full-time education. The pupil must also be supervised when doing activities outside of school within normal school hours, and if they feel that the person is not suitable to provide such a role they can refuse to approve the activity. Some schools operate a policy of issuing out-of-school passes so that pupils who have been authorized for flexi-schooling do not get into trouble for truancy.

Flexi-schooling presents a bit of a problem to schools because it is then up to their Local Authority to determine whether a pupil is entitled to the full amount of funding due to the days that a pupil is absent from the school. They may decide to pay the school on a pro rata basis and only pay for the days that the pupil is present at the school. The head teacher will need to consider this when asked if a pupil can do flexi-schooling.

In most cases where a head teacher grants flexi-schooling the pupil will be older and will be studying towards a vocational qualification or a qualification that is not available within that particular school. This could be anything from attending a drama class to working towards a specialist subject such as animal care. In some cases where a child has found it unbearable to go to school, a sympathetic head teacher may agree to keep the pupil on the school register and allow him/her to study the same subjects at home as they would normally do in school but via a distance learning programme. However, this is quite rare and a head teacher wouldn't allow every child to do this.

There are both advantages and disadvantages to flexi-schooling. The advantages can be that children benefit from a broader range of learning and can specialize in subjects that they might not be able to study at school. Parents also have a greater input into their children's education, but can also work flexi-time with their own jobs – something many parents that home educate can't do. Children also have shorter school weeks, but can still maintain the friendships they have made with classmates. The disadvantages of flexi-schooling can be that they might lose the closeness they have with classmates because they are in and out of school all the time. They might find that the days that they are not in school, they miss out on some important information and may feel that they then need to catch up. They might also get teased on the days they are in school for being different.

Case study: The best of both worlds

'I've always been passionate about horses and spend all my spare time having riding lessons. I know exactly what I want to do when I leave school and that is to open my own specialist riding school in Italy, for horse owners who want to learn dressage. I still want to take my GCSEs but I also want to get my British Horse Society (BHS) qualifications. There are four stages for the BHS exams I want to take, plus the teaching qualifications, and I can't start my school until I have these.

My parents asked my head teacher if I would be allowed out of school two days a week to study for my BHS exams and fortunately she agreed. She knows how passionate I am about horses and knows that unless I start now, I will have to spend another three years after I leave school just to study the subject and take these exams.

I go to school on Monday, Tuesday and Wednesday and the rest of the time I go to a private equestrian school where I learn everything needed for my BHS exams. It's hard work keeping up with my school work and taking my exams at the same time, and I sometimes feel as though I'm missing out on what's been going on at school because I'm only there three days a week, but really I have the best of both worlds. I've already taken my BHS stage 1 exam and I am working towards my BHS stage 2, but I'm not allowed to take that until I am 16. I already have my Riding and Road Safety Test exam and I am looking forward to the day when I can have my own riding school!'

Jade, 15, flexi-schooling student

Distance learning

Distance learning is another option for older children who study better on their own than in a class. Distance learning is exactly what it says; it is learning at a distance, and this is something many home educators consider when home schooling older children. Many older children who are home educated often feel that they need to gain recognized qualifications – in England and Wales these are the General Certificate of Secondary Education or GCSEs – but do not want to go to school in order to do this. This is where distance learning comes into play. It is an ideal way to learn from home as well as being able to gain recognizable qualifications in order to gain entry into a college of further education or for entry into an apprenticeship.

Many distance-learning colleges such as the National Extension College and Oxford Home Schooling offer academic courses in GCSEs and A Levels that can be studied from home. You are usually allocated your own tutor and many distance-learning colleges now offer discounts for children who are educated from home. Most distance learning colleges don't organize a place for you to sit your exams, so you have to find out where your nearest exam centre is, apply as a private student and pay the exam fee separately from your course.

The advantage of taking a distance-learning course is that very often children can take exams much earlier than their peers – students generally complete the courses quicker than school pupils for each particular subject. Another advantage is that all the materials that they will need to study a subject will be included in the fee, so there are no additional expenses other than the exam fee.

The disadvantages of taking qualifications by distance learning are that if you don't understand something you might have to wait for a response from your tutor. Usually they are very good, and will email you back within a day or two, but sometimes you might find that you are stuck on a section of work and your tutor is on holiday or away sick. Another disadvantage is the fact that the courses are not cheap. At around £350 per GCSE and £400 per A level, this can work out quite expensive if you are planning to take several exams. Many school children take between six and 12 GCSEs at school which is all funded by the government. If you were to allow your child to take the same, it would cost you a small fortune. However, one other advantage to counter this is that children that are home educated generally take GCSEs and A Levels at any age, so they can start much earlier than schoolchildren.

Distance learning is ideal if your child works well on his/her own and many courses come with additional online learning tools and materials. However, if your child doesn't work well on his/her own, you may find that you have to study the subject first and help them when it comes to coursework.

Subject choice

The subjects that most distance-learning colleges cover are:

GCSEs

- Biology
- Business studies
- Chemistry
- Child development
- English language
- English literature
- French
- Geography
- History
- Human physiology and health
- ICT
- ICT short course – upgrade to a full GCSE
- Law
- Maths foundation
- Maths higher
- Physics
- Psychology
- Science
- Sociology
- Spanish.

A Levels

- Accounting
- Biology
- Business studies
- Classical civilization
- Critical thinking
- Economics
- English language and literature
- English literature
- Environmental studies
- French
- Geography
- Government and politics
- History

- Law
- Mathematics
- Philosophy
- Psychology
- Religious studies
- Sociology.

It is also possible to study several subjects at a time and many children split their week into the subjects that they are studying. So long as finances are not an issue for you then this is an ideal way of educating your child if you want them to be home educated but at the same time you want him/her to leave education with some recognizable qualifications.

Top tip

Check several course providers and colleges – many will offer discounts for online bookings or for home-educated children.

Case study: Distance learning and qualifications

'I've been home educated all my life, so I don't know what it's like to be taught in a classroom or in a school, but I don't think I've missed out at all. From what I've seen, kids don't get to do anything they want to at school and have to do lessons whether or not they like them.

I love English literature and in particular the classics, so that's what I decided to study by distance learning. I started off with three GCSEs when I was 13 – English literature, English and History and I passed them all with good grades. When I was 14 I decided to take two more and passed psychology and business studies. This year I'm going to try to do two A Levels – one in English literature and one in Economics. If I pass them both I will have two A Levels by the time I'm 16. I then plan to take a year or two out and go travelling with my family and then hopefully go to university to study a degree in English.

I enjoy learning on my own, but I've also had some really nice tutors that have helped me. The scariest bit for me is going into an exam centre with all these people that are much older than me, but I usually cope OK and I always take Scruff, a soft toy dog my mum bought me for my first exam and my lucky mascot.

I would say that if you want to go to college and need exams to get in, then this is an ideal way to study for them. They cost quite a bit, but because we are with the charity Education Otherwise we can get a discount on most of the courses. Exams are also good to have if you are thinking of going straight into a job because nowadays employers like to see that you have been studying hard. Also it's a good personal achievement. I never thought I would enjoy working towards and taking exams, but it keeps me focussed and means that I'm not tempted to stay in bed all day because I know that I have to send my assignments off to my tutor!'

Sarah-Louise, 16, distance learner

Tutor-based learning

Some home educators hire private tutors to teach their children. Whilst this idea is very appealing and an excellent way to teach your children subjects that perhaps you do not know anything about or don't have the will to learn, it is a costly option.

Private tuition starts from around £30 per hour and if you are not planning on teaching anything to your child yourself, it will be very expensive to have a tutor in for every single subject that your child studies.

Many university students advertize private tuition for subjects that they have previously studied and this is often a cheaper option for many parents. A lot of parents hire a private tutor to teach certain core subjects such as maths and English. Others will pay for specialist private lessons such as learning a musical instrument or studying a more specialist subject, such as ice skating lessons.

If money is no problem then you might consider hiring in a private tutor for all your child's lessons. Years ago, education at home was only for the privileged that could afford it and parents would employ a governess who would teach their children every subject. This soon led to the introduction of private schools where, for a fee, children would be given a better education than the one that the state could provide – smaller class sizes, individual lessons and more choice in the subjects they could learn.

Key points

- There are many different styles of learning; the ones covered in this chapter are just a few.
- You do not have to follow the National Curriculum if you do not wish to.
- Distance learning is an option if your child wishes to work towards exams.

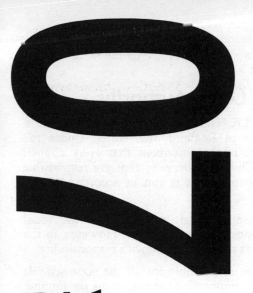

07

you and your Local Authority

In this chapter you will learn:

- what the Local Authority do
- how to talk to your Local Authority
- how to keep records of your child's work
- what a School Attendance Order is.

Those who know how to think need no teachers.

Mahatma Gandhi

The role of the Local Authority

A Local Authority, or LA, is responsible for the education within a particular area in England and Wales. Under the Children Act 2004 there is a requirement that every council appoints a Director of Children's Services that are responsible for ensuring that their department is run in accordance with the jurisdiction.

In London, the London borough councils are the local authorities that are responsible for education. However, in the metropolitan counties it is the county council's responsibility.

The Local Authorities are responsible for all the state schools within their area. They are responsible for organizing the funding for each school, allocating place numbers and employing staff and teachers. Voluntary-aided or privately-funded schools are responsible for employing their own staff. Local Authorities are also responsible for allocating places to pupils and ensuring that children registered at a school attend that school. Unfortunately, whilst some Local Authorities are up to date with issues regarding home education, many have been supplied with little information and surprisingly there are some that still believe that it is illegal to educate your children from home and are not equipped with the knowledge of the Education Act.

Like Iris Harrison and her family, a number of parents have been threatened with court or having their children taken away by LA officers and unless they are forewarned about their rights, have accepted what the LA officer says to be true. This is not always the case. Your child must be educated, but school is not compulsory.

There have also been a number of LA officers that claim that they have every right to enter your home and check up on your children if you choose to home educate them. There have been tragic situations like the case involving Victoria Climbie, the little girl who was never sent to school and who was mistreated by her family and subsequently died as a result of their neglect. However, any Local Authority or Education Welfare Officer who uses this kind of example as an excuse to check up on your children is abusing their position. Although Victoria Climbie did not go to school, she was not home educated. It was also made obvious from the investigation into her death that the Social Services and other authorities were involved in her welfare and the care that her guardians were supposed to be giving to her. If a person suspects that a child is being abused or neglected then those concerns are reported and investigated by Social Services, not a Local Authority. There is no legal basis for your LA to insist on visiting you and your child at home just because you are home educating. If they were concerned about your child's welfare, they should contact the local Social Services team who will take up the case.

> **Top tip**
>
> The better prepared and informed you are of your rights, the better you will be able to answer any questions the Local Education Officer might have.

Knowing your role and your rights

One of the primary aims of the LA is to ensure that every child of school age is receiving an education in relation to his/her age and ability. Because an education is generally thought of as the National Curriculum and only one that a school can provide, LA officers are often bemused by the freedom of home education and can sometimes wrongly advise parents of what is a suitable education. Many parents have come under attack by the LAs because they feel that unless a child is being taught in accordance with every other child in the country, the parents are not providing an adequate education for that child. Nowhere within the Education Act does it specify what you must and must not teach your child, nor does it state what a suitable education is. The only criteria a parent must meet if they decide to educate their child from home is that they do provide an education – meaning that children are not left on their own and that the parent is in charge of their child's education – and that the education they receive is suitable to the child's age and ability. It does not specify exactly what determines an education.

The charity Education Otherwise reports that this is one of the biggest issues they are asked about and often have to intervene when a Local Authority has misinformed a parent about their rights to educate their child.

To clarify, under section 7 of the Education Act 1996, a parent has a responsibility to provide their child with an efficient and full-time education suitable to his/her age and ability. This education does not have to be in accordance with what a school teaches nor does it have to include the National Curriculum.

The LA only has a duty to act if it appears that a parent is not providing an education to their child. For example, if they are informed that a child is left at home on their own or is spending their days wandering the streets, or is seen to be working in a place of employment, rather than learning.

Although the LA often request to visit a family that is educating their child/children from home, a parent is not legally obliged to accept this and is not obliged to respond to these type of requests. Nor is a parent legally required to provide or offer proof of the education that they are providing their child. Although it could be seen as not providing an education by not responding to any enquiries from the LA, you are not legally bound to prove yourself or respond to any enquiries from them. I personally have never had a problem with our Local Authority or our home-educating officer. In fact, she has been very helpful to me and the children.

Most Local Authorities will initially send a letter with a form enclosed which requests you to fill in details of how you intend to educate your child. Again, you are not legally obliged to provide any details to the LA. They cannot prove that you are not sufficiently educating your child purely on the absence of information. You are under no obligation to meet anyone from the LA, accept visits to your home, or keep them informed of your child's progress and the education you provide does not have to be academic, does not have to follow any curriculum, nor do you have to match school standards. Added to this, any work that your child completes is his or her own personal property and you are not at liberty to send it to anyone for assessment without your child's permission.

The problem many home-educating parents find is that Local Authorities seem only able to accept that an education is an education only if a child is following the National Curriculum and matching school-based targets. They often fail to see that an 'education' is a very broad range. If a child shows an interest in a subject that is not covered by the National Curriculum, for example ice skating, and only wants to learn that subject, that child is still receiving a suitable education. Just because a child isn't learning what every other child his/her age is learning, it does not mean that he/she isn't receiving an education.

It is not up to the LA to dictate what passes as a suitable education and it is not their job to say whether the education you provide to your child is deemed satisfactory or not. The only time they are legally allowed to act is if they believe that you are not providing a full-time education to your child/children and, as with Iris Harrison's case, they would have to prove this in a court of law. It is then up to the court to decide whether or not you are providing a sufficient education to your child in relation to their age, ability and any special needs they might have.

Case study: My experience with the LA

When I was first contacted by my LA it was by letter and they enclosed a form for me to fill out as to what I intended to teach my daughter. Because I wasn't fully aware of my rights, I meticulously filled it out, detailing everything that I intended to teach her and posted it back. This I now feel was a mistake because it left me open to proving that I was actually teaching what I had written on the form, when actually some subjects that my daughter was initially enthusiastic about have been dropped in favour of other more exciting subjects.

Once the LA had received my form, they wrote to me again to arrange a home visit. Although we have nothing to hide, I didn't realize that I was within my rights to refuse a home visit and I didn't legally have to oblige. As it turned out the LA officer was a very nice lady who was pro-home educating and didn't tell me what I should and shouldn't be doing. We now have a visit once a year, which usually consists of a cup of tea and an informal chat with me and the children.

Top tip

Believe it or not, Local Authority Officers are humans too! Sometimes they are not fully aware of the laws relating to education. Be confident but friendly and you will soon have them on your side.

Proof of work

Although you are not obliged to prove to anyone what your child has been doing at home, many parents, myself included, do keep all their work just in case educational rules ever change and we need to prove to someone that my children are receiving an adequate education.

As mentioned before, you do not have to follow the National Curriculum and therefore do not have to show that your child's work is in line with that or any other curriculum. Just as every child is different, so too is every home-educating family and their style of learning. One of my daughters loves nothing more than painting and writing stories – she has already penned her first novel which she is planning to get published – and yet my other daughter is more academic and prefers to work through a maths or a science book.

If they are doing something creative such as making models out of clay for example, I will take a digital photo of the finished product and store it in what I call my 'proof book'. Some subjects such as sports are of course impossible to record in a book, so I also try to keep a weekly/fortnightly diary of what activities they have undertaken. Some weeks we won't do any academic or written work at all, and might spend the whole week out and about going ice skating, climbing or orienteering and then camping in the woods, which is hard to keep a record of, so on weeks like this I just write it in the 'proof diary'.

If you are happy for an LA officer to visit you and your child at home, remember that you do not have to answer any questions that you feel are inappropriate or make you feel uncomfortable. I would like to say that all a LA officer wants to do is make sure that your child is receiving a suitable education to their age and ability, but unfortunately this is not the case for every LA officer. Some are opposed to home schooling and feel that all children should be in a school environment. Perhaps some expect you to turn your home into a classroom, with your child sitting at a desk, workbooks at the ready.

Many home educators who follow an autonomous style of learning don't tend to work this way. To the untrained it might look like your child is just watching the TV or playing in the garden, but children are learning from the moment they wake up until the moment they go to bed. Just because a child isn't sitting behind a desk doesn't mean that he/she isn't learning anything. Very often if you ask a child at school what they have been doing all day you will receive the stock answer of a shrug of the shoulders and a reply of 'nothing much'. Can you imagine a LA officer's reaction if this was the answer to the same question of a home-educated child? Unfortunately, we feel under more pressure to ensure that our children are learning than the parents that drop their children off at the school gate and let the teachers get on with it. Added to this, if a child is given a relatively free rein as to what they would like to learn about, they tend to *want* to learn the subject, rather than feel that they are being *forced* to learn it.

> **Top tip**
>
> Why not get your older children to design a website/blog about their education, what better proof of a child's learning than from the child themselves?

Tracking progress

At the end of a school year I tend to go through the children's work and write up an annual report of what they have achieved during the course of that year. Again, this is not a requirement, nor is it something that the LA requests. Partly for me it is so that if anyone in authority asks me to prove that I am educating my children sufficiently I can provide them with a copy of my report. It is also good for the children to see how much progress they have made and what they have covered in the course of a year.

Even if you don't do any academic work, everything a child does can be written in what I like to call 'teacher-jargon'. So, for example, an afternoon spent playing an online computer strategy game can come under the categories of maths (working out graphs and dimensions, cross grid references etc.), hand/eye co-ordination skills, reading skills (reading game instructions), writing skills (issuing instructions), brain training (keeping up with your opponents), IT skills (using a computer effectively), social skills (interacting with an opponent). All these skills are being learned as your child plays a game they enjoy and they are learning without realizing it. I do stress here that it is not imperative that you keep records. It is a matter of personal choice.

School Attendance Orders

Whilst you are under no obligation to meet with or prove to the LA that you are providing a sufficient education for your children, if your Local Authority thinks that your child is not receiving an education suitable to his/her age and ability, they may issue you with what is known as a School Attendance Order or SAO. The LA cannot automatically issue a SAO and have to give you the opportunity to supply them with the information they have asked from you – this could be anything from proof that your child is receiving an education to proof that you are not leaving your child at home all day on his/her own. If the LA is still not satisfied, they have to give you 15 days notice that a School Attendance Order will be issued to you.

If for example your child has been seen working on a market stall seven days a week, you would not be providing that child with a suitable education in accordance to his/her age and ability. The same as if your child was found to be busking on the streets or driving around in a tractor all day. You would first be asked by the LA to supply information to prove that your child is at home and learning at home and if the LA were still not satisfied, you would be issued with a School Attendance Order.

In the SAO they have to inform you which school they intend your child to attend. It will also inform you of the date you must register your child at that school and the reasons why the LA feels that you are not providing your child with a proper and full-time education.

If you are issued with a SAO you must not ignore it. If you do, you could face a fine or be taken to court. As in the case of the Harrisons, if you are providing your children with an education that is in line with their age and ability and you are faced with a tyrant of an LA officer, you should call in a lawyer who knows about home education – the charity Education Otherwise can put you in touch with someone. You will then be required by law to provide evidence that your child is receiving an education and will be asked by the court to provide samples of work, photographs, a diary or other evidence. The court will then be able to assess whether or not your child is receiving an education in line with his/her age, ability and any special needs he/she might have.

It is rare that you will receive a SAO if you are educating your child from home efficiently and effectively.

Key points

* Although you may be perfectly happy to accept a home visit from an LA officer, you are under no obligation to do so.
* Whilst you do not have to keep records of your child's progress, it is nice for them, and for you, to see how they have improved.
* Your Local Authority is responsible for ensuring that all children of school age are educated to a standard in accordance with their learning ability and their age.

08

socialization

In this chapter you will learn:
- about studies into socialization and home-educated children
- suggestions for socialization.

All men who have turned out worth anything have had the chief hand in their own education.

Sir Walter Scott

Socialization issues

This is one of the main concerns that parents face when deciding whether or not to educate their children from home. Many worry that their child/children will suffer as a result of not being in school with other children their own age and will become recluses. Much research has been conducted in relation to home-educated children and socialization and there is no evidence to suggest that a home-educated child misses out socially.

Humans are naturally social creatures and will naturally relate to people. It is assumed that just because home-educated children are not interacting with other children for half an hour in a playground, that they are not socializing and are missing out. Research has found that a home-educated child is just as likely, if not more so, to be sociable with the people he/she meets than school children in a class of 30 plus.

Just because a child goes to school it doesn't necessarily mean that they are any more sociable than a child that doesn't. This was demonstrated in an article in the *Guardian*, 02nd May 2006, when MP Graham Allen told Westminster that, children in one of the most deprived areas of Britain could barely read let alone converse with one another and were in dire need of being taught social skills. Mr Allen said that, 'We need to train the parents of tomorrow and end the feelings of anti-education or we will never have good levels of attainment.' He stated that 11 per cent of 11 year olds in his constituency could not read when they entered secondary school and that the children's communication and social skills were appalling.

Schoolchildren will have social skills that are very different to those of a home-educated child. They may be able to converse with their peers but often not with people outside of their age group. Home-educated children tend to mix and interact naturally with all sorts of people. In general they are more confident than a child who is only allowed to mix with other children of the same age because they have been allowed to mix with people of all ages, ethnicities, religions and socio-economic backgrounds.

It is a misconception that children who are educated at home sit at a desk on their own from 9 a.m. to 3 p.m. and spend their day isolated and alone. This couldn't be further from the truth. Every home educator that I know is out and about with their child/children most days, visiting museums, taking art classes, drama classes, going to Guides or Scouts, or travelling the world. Dr Raymond Moore, the author of over 60 books and articles on the development of humans, has compiled extensive research on children that are educated from home and says 'the idea that children need to be around other children in a bid for socialization is perhaps the most dangerous myth in education and raising children today.'

Dr Moore's study showed that in general children often do not work well in large groups. Learning becomes difficult and there is no room for individualism because the more dominant children in a large group easily influence the behaviour of the other children. In a study of over 8,000 children, Dr Moore concluded that children are best socialized by their parents and not other children. He also questions what kind of socialization happens when there are 30 children of the same age range in a classroom day after day. Peer pressure is huge and children feel that they have to look and behave the same as every other child in the group for fear of being labelled as different, which in turn means that they never discover who they really are. How many times have you heard someone say that a child is a 'typical teenager'? How sad that every teenager in the country is labelled in this way.

> **Top tip**
>
> As home education increases, more groups of home-educated children are being set up. These are ideal places for both you and your child to get together with other like-minded people.

Evidence and research

In July 2000, the Discovery Institute in America published a report about home education which was written by Senior Fellow Dr Patricia Lines. The institute conducted many controlled studies to compare the social skills of home-educated children with state-funded schoolchildren. The home-educated children rated as being well-adjusted children. In one particular study researchers watched videos of mixed groups of home-educated children and state-schooled children playing. The home-educated children were found to have fewer behavioural problems than those who attended school. Dr Lines concluded that there was no basis to question the social development of home-educated children.

A report written by Chris Klicka, the Senior Counsel for the Home School Legal Defense Association, stated that schoolchildren were not being given the chance to socialize properly. Klicka said that schoolchildren were trapped within a group of children for at least 190 days each year with little or no opportunity to be exposed to other children of other ages or adults. The adults that they were exposed to were seen to be the 'enemy'. The children were given little or no responsibility and everything was provided for them. Klicka found that children that were educated at home did not have these problems because they were exposed to the real world, could relate easily to adults and learn in a more hands-on way than children that were simply prepared to remember a set of facts and be tested on them in order to achieve a grade.

Assistant Professor of Education of Michigan, J. Gary Knowles, compiled a study at the University of Michigan which found that teaching children at home did not make them social misfits. Knowles surveyed 53 adults who were taught at home and found that two-thirds were married, which is the norm for adults their age, none were unemployed and three-quarters said that they felt that being taught at home had helped them to interact with people from different levels of society. He also found that more than 40 per cent attended college and 15 per cent of those had completed a graduate degree. Nearly two-thirds were self-employed. Professor Knowles said that the fact that so many home-educated children went into self-employment suggested that home schooling tended to enhance a person's self-reliance, confidence and independence. In the study, 96 per cent of the home-educated adults said that given the choice they would want to be taught at home again.

> **Top tip**
>
> Studies have shown that children lose their individualism in large groups. Your child will not suffer if they are not always socializing with children of their own age.

How to ensure your child socializes

Some people have suggested that it is easier for a child to be home educated if he/she has siblings that are also educated at home and that it is more difficult for an only child to socialize. In some respects this is true, if a child has siblings at home they can engage in conversations, discuss debates and play together. However, an only child can do all these things with his/her parents or other home-educated friends and school friends.

If you are worried about isolation here are a few suggestions to ensure your child socializes with other people:

- Find out if there are other home educators in your area. Your Local Education Authority should have a list of other home educators and home-educating organizations. If they don't, then visit the Education Otherwise website (see Chapter 11). You will find a list of groups local to you.
- Find home-educating groups on the Internet and join their chat rooms. All home-educating group members are checked for your child's safety as well as your own.
- Enrol your child in an after-school club such as Guides, Scouts, drama lessons, dance classes etc. This way they will make friends outside of the house.
- When you meet families out with their children during school hours, ask them if they home educate their children.
- If your children used to go to school, encourage them to stay in touch with their old friends. Invite them round on weekends or have sleepovers on holidays.
- Many councils have after-school sports programmes and local park events during the school holidays. This is an ideal way for your children to meet other children.

Children get bored easily and have a natural instinct to socialize. If you watch a child visiting a park or a children's activity venue you will notice that in no time at all one will walk up to another and ask them if they want to play. They are not concerned about whether they go to school, don't go to school, what their favourite music is or anything else. My six-year-old daughter very wisely told me one day, 'If you want to make friends with someone mummy, you should just go up to them and say, "Would you like to be my friend?"'

Given the opportunity children will happily mix with other children of all ages and abilities, so there is no need to worry about whether your child is going to miss out on the social aspects if they no longer go to school.

Case study: Keeping old friends and making new ones

'Socialization was one of the main things that worried me when we took Josh out of school. Although he was a quiet child, he always had a lot of school friends and was very popular, so I wondered whether he was going to miss out not having his friends to play with everyday. In fact, that was the only thing he said he would miss about school.

When Josh left school we made sure we had all his friends' phone numbers and I encouraged him to phone them in the evenings and at weekends. He also had most of his friends as messenger buddies on the Internet, so he was able to keep in touch with them every evening if he wasn't out playing.

Because Josh is an only child and I am a single mum, I made sure that he joined as many clubs and organizations as possible. I couldn't afford to pay for some of the more expensive clubs, but discovered that the local library was a valuable source of all sorts of activities that he could try and where he could meet new people.

I work part time as a community nurse and Josh often comes with me to the surgery and sits in the waiting room doing his work while I see patients. On one occasion he got talking to a deaf lady who started to teach him how to sign. Josh said he would like to volunteer at the young person's deaf centre where the lady worked and he now visits there once a week and helps out. He is learning British Sign Language and has made lots more friends his own age.

Although we live in a small village, there is a group of home educators that meet once a month in the city, which is about 20 miles away, so we often meet up for events or even just to play in the park. I don't think that Josh misses out at all. It's just as though he goes to another school. In fact, our weekends are always busy with his friends coming to stay and the holidays are no different to when he was at school. I needn't have worried about him. Josh is much more sociable now than he ever was at school and we now have some very in-depth conversations, which is something we never used to do.'

Kate, home-educating mum to Josh, 13

Top tip

If you have an only child encourage him/her to socialize with people of all ages, join after-school clubs or get involved in charity organizations.

Key points

- Encourage your child to mix with children that go to school and other home-educated children.
- There is no evidence to say that home education is detrimental to a child's ability to socialize.

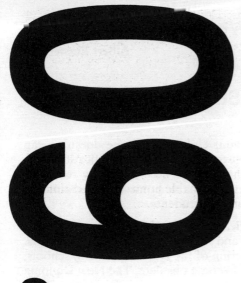

09

qualifications

I never teach my pupils; I only attempt to provide the conditions in which they can learn.

Albert Einstein

Studying for GCSEs, A Levels and the New Diploma

Just because you educate your child from home doesn't mean that your child won't be able to take the same qualifications that a child in a traditional school can. There are many resources available to home educators that enable home-educated children to take qualifications as external students.

At present, the main qualifications taken by state-funded school pupils aged between 14 and 19 are GCSEs and A Levels. However, with the introduction of the New Diploma in schools, GCSEs and A Levels could become obsolete. The New Diploma will be qualified in three tiers: A Foundation Diploma will be equivalent to taking five GCSE grades D to G; a Higher Diploma will be equivalent to seven GCSEs, grades A* to C; and the Advanced Diploma will be the same as gaining 3.5 A Levels.

At the time of writing, state-funded schools are still offering GCSEs and A Levels, but have started to introduce the New Diploma into their syllabus, which is going to be part of the national programme for all state-funded schools. The aim is that the Diplomas will eventually cover 17 subjects and all students studying for a Diploma will have to achieve the minimum standard in English, maths and ICT, and complete a minimum of ten days' work experience.

A home-educated child can gain a recognized qualification in the same way as an adult/mature learner could. There are many external colleges such as the National Extension College, Sheffield College and The Open Learning Centre International that offer GCSE and A Level courses to home-educated pupils, and many offer a small discount to those that learn from home. Sheffield College have specially designed their GCSE courses for students aged 14 years and up so that they work predominately via the Internet.

Some distance learning colleges provide the materials for a specific course but you then have to register your child as an external student for his/her exam. Others will include the exam fee and register your child for you. Once your child has studied the course material for a particular qualification you will have to find a venue in which to sit the actual exam. Most of the examining boards will provide a list of locations where the exams will take place, and will detail whether or not they accept private/external candidates. The syllabus for all GCSE exams are part of the National Curriculum and will be the same for every examining board across the country. A full list of exam centres can be found at the AQA examining board's website, **www.aqa.org.uk.** The AQA have previous GCSE and A Level papers that you can download for free and in most cases will mark coursework for a student whose exam includes coursework. At the time of writing the costs for taking a GCSE exam as an external student are between £20 and £25 per subject.

Many of the distance learning colleges offer courses that are not part of the National Curriculum, for example vocational courses such as counselling, alternative health, animal care etc., and will inform you of where your nearest exam centre is. In time it is believed that many of the colleges that offer GSCE and A Level courses will also offer the New Diploma courses to their students. As a private student this might involve the student having to arrange their own work experience for the hands-on part of the course.

Many parents of home-educated children have questioned whether they should bother taking GCSE and A Level courses if their child's school peers are going to be studying for Diplomas and colleges and universities are going to accept the Diploma as an entry requirement. At the time of writing, GCSE and A Level courses will continue to be taught until at least 2013, although many of them will be updated. The idea of introducing the New Diploma and a number of Apprenticeships is to enable pupils to study a qualification which suits their interests and learning style. Just as many parents of home-educated children will have left school with either CSEs or O Levels (which are now the equivalent to the modern GCSE), GCSEs and A Levels will still be recognized by employers, colleges and universities.

The International GCSE

The International GCSE (IGCSE), which is primarily aimed at foreign students wishing to take GCSEs abroad, is now available to private schools and home educators. To gain the

IGCSE you do not have to submit coursework and it is an internationally recognized qualification. The subjects you can study for the IGCSE include:

- Accounting
- Afrikaans – First language
- Afrikaans – Second language
- Agriculture
- Arabic – First language
- Arabic – Foreign language
- Art and design
- Bangladeshi studies
- Biology
- Business studies
- Chemistry
- Child development
- Chinese (Mandarin) – Foreign language
- Chinese – First language
- Computer studies
- Czech – First language
- Design and technology
- Development studies
- Drama
- Dutch – First language
- Dutch – Foreign language
- Economics
- English – First language
- English – Literature
- English – Second language
- Environmental management
- Food and nutrition
- French – First language
- French – Foreign language
- Geography
- German – First language
- German – Foreign language
- Global Perspectives
- Greek – Foreign language
- Hindi as a Second language
- History
- Indonesian – Foreign language

- Information and communication technology
- Information technology
- IsiZulu – Second language
- Japanese – First language
- Japanese – Foreign language
- Korean – First language
- Latin
- Malay – Foreign language
- Mathematics
- Mathematics (with coursework)
- Mathematics – Additional
- Cambridge international mathematics
- Music
- Pakistani studies
- Physical education
- Physical science
- Physics
- Portuguese – First language
- Portuguese – Foreign language
- Religious studies
- Russian – First language
- Science – Combined
- Sciences – Coordinated (double)
- Sociology
- Spanish – First language
- Spanish – Foreign language
- Spanish – Literature
- Thai – First language
- Travel and tourism
- Turkish – First language
- Twenty-First century science.

The exam board Edexcel, formed in 1996 by the merger of the Business and Technology Education Council (BTEC), the country's leading provider of vocational qualifications, and the University of London Examinations and Assessment Council (ULAC), one of the major exam boards for GCSEs and A levels, welcomes students from all walks of life, including home-educated children. Again, you have to pay for course materials and tutoring, and at present there are only a few centres where exams can be sat. Details of these can be found at the Edexcel website, **www.edexcel.com**

Top tip
The Open University offer many free online courses.

Further education colleges

Many colleges will now take students from the age of 14 and upwards on their full- and part-time courses. However, this very much depends on the college you approach. Some have autonomous units which welcome young students while others provide science courses specifically for home-educated pupils. Some colleges work in conjunction with their Local Education Authority and local schools on a pupil referral system where it has been shown that a pupil has experienced problems being educated in a school. Funding is always provided by the LA in referral cases because a pupil is still registered at a state-funded school.

Some colleges will not admit pupils that are under the age of 16. Some Local Authorities are under the impression that colleges are not allowed to take students who are under 16, but the decision is up to the principal of the college and not the LA.

Entry into college

Some parents are concerned about entry qualifications when their children reach 16 and qualify for further education. Many courses state that they require a number of GCSEs in order to gain acceptance onto a course of further education, others however, are happy with just some evidence of a student's ability or will accept a new student after an interview.

If your son or daughter doesn't have GCSEs I would recommend that they create a portfolio of their best bits of work that they are most proud of as an example of their ability to stick with the course they have chosen. Most colleges realize that not every child is going to come with the standard four GCSEs grade C or above and will happily accept students who can show that they are hard working and interested in the course. Even universities now offer Access courses for students that might not have the relevant A Levels.

> **Top tip**
>
> Many colleges will accept your child with no formal qualifications.

Another viable option is that if you are interested in studying the same course that your child is interested in studying, you as a parent could enrol on a college course and allow your child to study the work. Again, you would need to check with your local college about whether your child could enter any exams as an external student.

> **Top tip**
>
> Many colleges offer free courses or taster sessions. Check with your local college.

Costs

Because you have chosen to take your child out of the state-funded school system and stated that you intend to educate your child from home, your Local Authority are not obliged to offer funding for your child's education, unless you are in the situation where your child is still registered at a state-funded school. When I contacted my local college to enquire whether my daughter could study a BTEC certificate in Business Studies I was told that I would have to pay the course fees until she was 16 when she would then get further education funding. At the time of writing, LAs have confirmed that they are only prepared to pay for pre-16s to attend college in exceptional circumstances. So, as with studying for National Curriculum exams, if a college of further education accepts your child as a student, you will have to pay the college fees until your child reaches the age of 16. Some colleges have concerns about whether their insurance covers under 16s so this is another thing to consider when asking a college if they take young students.

Some home-educated children have left school because of issues of bullying or situations arising from them requiring a special needs education. If this is the case and you wish your child to go to a college of further education, it would be worth speaking with your Local Education Authority Officer about the option of still being registered as a pupil at his/her school, but being offered their education at the local college before you de-register your child.

> **Top tip**
>
> Keep some of your child's best work and create a portfolio for them should they decide they wish to go to college. Some colleges will accept a portfolio instead of formal qualifications.

Modern apprenticeships

Years ago the norm was to leave school and go straight into an apprenticeship – this is how many of our best engineers started out. An apprenticeship provides on-the-job training but also enables the apprentice to earn a wage and study for a recognized qualification such as an NVQ at the same time.

Today they are called Modern Apprenticeships and there are currently over 180 apprenticeships across more than 80 industries. These can vary from travel and tourism to health and beauty, engineering, construction, equestrian skills, and even some of the old, traditional trades such as silversmithing, carpentry and glassmaking.

At the time of writing, an apprentice must be paid at least £80 per week, although some industries pay more and you may be able to get help with travel and accommodation costs. As an employee, an apprentice is also entitled to 20 days holiday per year (plus bank holidays). There are two ways in which you can apply for an apprenticeship: you can contact the Apprenticeships website at **www.apprenticeships.org.uk** or go direct to an employer and ask if they would consider taking you on as an apprentice.

Apprenticeships are a mixture of on- and off-the-job training. On the job, you will work with a mentor learning skills on site. Off the job, you will spend time with a Learning provider, working towards a National Vocational Qualification (NVQ) at Level 2 or 3. The amount of time you'll spend studying varies, it can be anything from 100 to 1,000 hours over the course of your Apprenticeship, depending on your chosen profession.

All sorts of people apply for apprenticeships and there is no set entry requirement for them, which makes it an ideal option for individuals that have been home educated. It means that you do not have to have a number of GCSEs in order to gain entry. The only requirements are that you must be living in England and not taking part in any full-time education.

Evening classes

There are many local colleges that offer evening courses for adults. However, some of them are somewhat reluctant to accept under 16s due to someone having to be present to be responsible for the child. Some colleges of further education will allow a child under the age of 16 to take an evening class as long as their parent is present, but again this is up to the individual college and funding for the course would be the responsibility of the parent.

Resources for younger children

There are many places that younger children can gain access to school resources including local libraries, which all have free Internet use, and local clubs that they can join. Since the increase in the number of home educators, more local groups are setting up all over the country. We currently live in a small rural village and it's a bit of a running joke that we are the only home educators in the village, however in the past year there have been two groups that have been set up by other home-educating parents, both within ten miles of the area where we live.

As part of the membership, the charity Education Otherwise will provide you with a list of any groups in your area and very often members will meet up with each other, usually once a month, and plan a whole month of activities that their children can participate in. More local activity and learning centres are becoming aware of home education and if you can get enough people interested they will give a good discount on entrance fees for a group booking. In our area we get a discount at the local ice rink if ten or more families attend a session at any one time, so it's worth getting together with other home-educating families and targeting places like science museums, theatres and other educational and sporting venues.

Top tip

Younger children love to role play so encourage them to set up a shop, a bank or a hairdressers. With a few large cardboard boxes, available free from your local store, they will have hours of fun creating their own little houses and shops.

Key points

- There are many resources available should your child wish to take nationally recognized exams, including local colleges and distance learning organizations.
- The International GCSE is a recognized qualification in the UK.
- Apprenticeships and evening classes are an alternative source of qualifications.

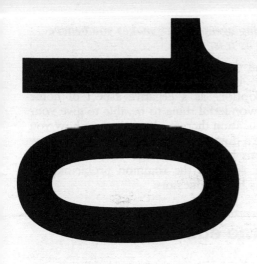

10

adapting to change

School is the advertising agency which makes you believe that you need society as it is.

I don't personally feel that there are any downsides to educating your children at home, but some may see issues such as restrictions to working options as a negative aspect of home schooling. Whilst it is a wonderful thing to be able to give your child the best possible education there is, depending on how you look at it, it can also have a down side. This chapter looks at how educating your child from home will change your life for the better, but also looks at some of the common problems that parents may experience as home educators.

The pros of home educating

Flexibility – no more early mornings

I know this is a small matter and not at the top of the list of reasons to educate your child at home, but I feel that it's worth mentioning. Schools do not have the option to be flexible in their hours of learning and most children have to start school at 9 a.m. and finish at 3 p.m. For older children who have to travel to school, mornings often start very early, sometimes as early as 7 a.m. if they have to catch a bus to school and they don't get home until after 5 p.m. On a practical level, these early starts often mean that a child has no time to have a leisurely breakfast before they start school and rush out of the house, bleary-eyed and ill-prepared for the day ahead of them. Many children that go to comprehensive school are out of the house for almost ten hours and will only eat at lunchtime.

Home educators don't have to rush around trying to catch buses or be at a lesson at a certain time which means that their day-to-day learning is a much more relaxed one right from the start. Learning often begins in an informal way at the breakfast table, perhaps with a discussion about an article in the morning newspaper, and will continue throughout the day and very often into the evening.

Any parent trying to get children out of bed and off to school will know that it is a very stressful job if not conducted with military precision – making sure that they all have their lunches, sports kits, signed notes for trips etc. Many an argument has broken out in my house over why one child is still finishing homework over a bowl of Coco Pops in the morning, whilst the other has forgotten to give me a list of ingredients for a cookery lesson that very morning!

When we started out on our venture of home educating I tried to stick with school times and hauled the children out of bed at 8 a.m., sat them down at desks, pencil in hand, ready to start their 'school' day. This lasted for all of one day. The following morning we overslept. From then on we decided to get up when we felt like it and we enjoyed a much more relaxed day of learning.

When you home educate you no longer have to be anywhere at a given time, unless of course you decide to go out for the day. There is none of that first-thing-in-the-morning stress that most parents have to go through every Monday through to Friday mornings and there is no rush to be back for 3.15 p.m. to pick the children up again.

Home educators can please themselves. Not everyone works best in the morning, so if you want to get up late, you can. If you want your children to discover what it's like for a nocturnal animal to live in the dark, you can sleep in all morning and venture out at night, armed with torches and even camping equipment if you so wish.

People who are used to our 'normal' structure of learning and education don't seem to realize that an education does not have to begin at 9 a.m. and end at 3 p.m. The flexibility of home education is wonderful and just one of the small advantages of being a home educator.

No more tears before bedtime

When my eldest daughter started school she spent every night in tears, telling me that she didn't want the morning to come because then she would have to go to school again. It wasn't any particular one thing that set her off and she wasn't school-phobic. It was a combination of having to get up early again, go into a classroom and stay there for the next six hours. When Friday came round she bounced out of the school gates, excited at the prospect of being able to have two whole days off and not having to go to school for any of them. Half terms and summer holidays were the times where she was most relaxed because she knew that she had a whole week or, in the case of the summer holidays, a whole six weeks, of doing as she pleased.

The worst day of the week was a Sunday evening when she would get upset at the prospect of going to school on the Monday. Invariably she would pretend she was poorly so that I would say that she was too ill to go to school and allowed her to stay at home. On one occasion when I wouldn't allow her another day off, she flatly refused to get out of bed. No amount of talking to her would persuade her to go to school so I had no choice but to rush my other daughter into school and make up an excuse to the headmaster that my other daughter had been sick in the car. During her school years, my daughter would suffer from migraines and I initially put this down to the fact that it was inherited from myself and my father. When she stopped going to school, the migraines stopped instantly and she has never had another one since. Since home educating my daughters we no longer get that 'Sunday evening dread'. Evenings are now relaxed and there is no stress within the house.

Learning what you want when you want

It seems ridiculous to me to be forced to learn a subject just because it's a requirement on the National Curriculum. What if you don't like that subject or are simply not interested in it? People could argue that a child should have access to a broad range of basic skills and information, which is really what the National Curriculum is all about – an introduction to the very basics of a subject. That is why they come out of school with a General Certificate of Secondary Education. And you could argue that if a child isn't given access to a subject how will they know whether they like it or not? However, we come across every subject in the National Curriculum in everyday life – a young child learns basic maths by working out how many sweets she can buy with the 50 pence her grandmother has given her; she will learn the effects of science when she mixes washing-up liquid with water and will learn Information Technology by playing computer games. Children will naturally be drawn to those subjects that are of particular interest to them.

The beauty of being educated at home is that your child is under no pressure to study subjects that don't interest them. It is true that the subjects we find most interesting are the subjects that we will easily excel in and want to study, rather than feeling we have to study a subject just for the sake of getting a basic knowledge about it. If, as an adult, you wanted to go to college or university and learn a new subject, you wouldn't choose something that you had no interest in, so why do we insist on making our children study subjects that they have no interest in?

Because home educating is somewhat 'out of the box' and not in line with what we regard as traditional learning in the form of the National Curriculum, people assume that a home-educated child is at a disadvantage if he/she doesn't stick with the 'tried and trusted' subjects of the National Curriculum. It's worth bearing in mind that the National Curriculum is only a range of subjects that is decided by the education department of the current government and as we have seen over the years, this can and has been changed with a change of government.

It's interesting that teachers have reported that by teaching children in a more relaxed and interesting way they learn at a faster rate and enjoy the lesson more than being taught by the traditional methods of teaching. A recent study by British education experts found that by providing pupils with the Nintendo Brain Training games the experts found that within just 20 minutes of a problem-solving session pupils outperformed those who were taught by traditional methods.

When your child is educated at home he/she is free to learn about the subjects that interest them most and learn when they want to. My children have chosen to work on projects in the evenings, weekends and even whilst we've been on holiday, simply because they are desperate to gain as much information about a subject as possible and it is no longer a chore to learn, but a pleasure. There is also the option of learning subjects that are not accessible in schools because they are not currently listed on the National Curriculum. To date my children have taken courses in photography, journalism and fashion design.

More family time

Unfortunately, we appear to be a nation where both parents need to work, children go to school and the only time we get to spend any quality time with our families is at the weekend, and even then most of the time is taken up with shopping, visiting relatives or doing out-of-school activities.

Home educating your child allows you to spend more time as a family. When my husband and I were both working full-time, our daughters were at school and then in after-school care for two hours every day; by the time we all got home and cooked dinner it was time for them to go to bed. We never really caught up with each other until the Sunday because my husband also had to work overtime on a Saturday. Sunday mornings were spent doing some activity, then we would visit relatives in the afternoon and in the evenings we were back to getting ready for work and school again. We hardly saw each other, let alone knew whether or not anyone had any problems.

Many parents tell me that they would love to be able to educate their children from home but that they need two incomes in order to keep the family afloat. Whilst I agree that most families nowadays need two incomes, it does not mean that you have to stick to the traditional 9 a.m. till 5 p.m. routine. The home-educating parents I know both have to work, but plan their work around their children's education and not the other way round. Some parents will work shifts so that there is always one at home to be the home educator; others will work from home or work part-time, fitting their hours around 'school' hours.

Holiday whenever you like

It is extremely annoying for families who are penalized by holiday companies because they are not allowed to take their children out of school during term time for a family holiday. A newspaper recently highlighted how parents were being fined up to £100 a time for taking their children on holiday during term time. Originally, head teachers were allowed to give up to ten days per year to pupils who wanted to take a holiday during term time, but in 2003 the government clamped down on unauthorized absences and gave Local Authorities the power to issue fines, take parents to court for non-attendance and they have also told schools not to allow term-time holidays. Tour operators and holiday companies often double their prices for holidays taken during half terms and school summer holidays because they know that this is the only time that families are allowed to take their vacation.

An advantage of being home educated means that if you want to go away for a week during what is considered by most as 'term time', you can, without having to obtain permission from the headmaster or waiting until the children's half term comes round – and pay double for the privilege.

Many home-educating families will use the experience of travelling in their learning; so a trip to France, for example, can not only be a relaxing holiday, it can also give your child a taste of French culture, cuisine, history and geography, among other things.

> **Top tip**
>
> HESFES (Home Education Seaside Festival) organizes an annual home-educators holiday by the sea. See Chapter 11 for more details.

Learning at your speed and at your level

School is designed to teach large numbers of pupils the same amount of information and at the same level. Therefore, it is impossible for those pupils that absorb information at a faster rate to learn any faster than the level at which everyone else is learning. A classroom teacher is only able to teach to a basic level (or Key Stage) of learning in any given subject because they must teach to the level required by the National Curriculum. The number of subjects pupils are taught means that teachers only have a limited amount of time to spend on each subject.

A home-educated child can spend as much or as little time on a subject as they choose. If they are studying a project about World War II and are eager to find out more about what life was really like for soldiers in the trenches, they can spend a month researching it. They are not limited to spending just an hour a week on the subject. If you notice that your child is more interested in photography than academic studies, he/she can spend all their time learning the craft and don't have to stop just because the lesson has ended. They can spend a year studying a City & Guilds certificate instead of just touching on a subject they love. They can also take GCSEs in all manner of subjects at any age as it gives a child the opportunity to learn at their own pace and not that dictated by a curriculum or timetable.

No uniform, no travel

Another advantage of home schooling your children is that you no longer have to buy school uniform or pay travel expenses. Where once a school uniform consisted of a white shirt and grey/black skirt or trousers, now many schools insist on slogan-based uniform, blazers, special sports socks that are only available from specialist suppliers and some may even insist on the same style of footwear.

I can accept the school of thought that if everyone is dressed the same then it prevents children from being the target of bullying and that children can be easily identified as belonging to a specific school, however in most areas of life people are allowed to dress as they choose. The only reason people wear a uniform is to inform the general public that they belong to an organization, i.e. the ambulance service, the police force, the army, the RSPCA etc.

The cost of a school uniform is a staggering amount and if you have several children this can run into hundreds of pounds a year. Added to this, many schools charge for the bus travel to and from school. These are two minor advantages of home educating your children, along with the fact that on a Sunday evening you are not desperately trying to wash, dry and iron several uniforms for the following day.

No peer pressure

Young people are under a lot of pressure to fit in, wear the same clothes as everyone else their age, listen to the same kind of music and do the same as their peers. Even if a child thinks something is wrong, it's hard to stand up and be the one to say so when everyone else is following the crowd. They can become ostracized for refusing to follow peer pressure. It takes a lot of self-confidence to walk away from something that you know is wrong, which is the reason why many children give in to peer pressure in the first place.

Home-educated children don't experience peer pressure because they are not in the situation where they feel that they have to be seen as being the same as every other child the same age. Studies have shown that children who are educated at home are less likely to start drinking or get into trouble with the police than those that are school educated because they do not feel any pressure from their peers to try to be the same. Many bullying issues arise from peer pressure and this is another reason why home education may be an ideal option for a child.

No more homework

I have never understood the concept of setting homework at school. Surely if children are being taught a subject properly, there shouldn't be the need for additional homework on a subject? I realize that the answer lies in the fact that a teacher is trying to teach a subject to 30 pupils at any one time and that the whole class has to learn at a set level. However, studies have shown that setting homework is not only a burden to both children and parents, but is also pointless. In most schools pupils are overloaded with homework and often have to stay up until the small hours of the morning in a bid to get it all done. This isn't right.

A leading UK private school decided to slash the amount of homework they set their pupils by 75 per cent, giving their pupils no more than 40 minutes a day. The results showed that the pupil's grades increased significantly. The principal of this particular school said that many of the tasks set as homework were meaningless and of no significant importance to the pupils. They were simply re-learning what they had been taught in class. As a home educator you no longer have to deal with making sure that homework is done and in on time and that takes the pressure off you and your child.

> **Top tip**
>
> There will be some aspects of school that your child might have enjoyed. For my two older girls it was creative time when they were allowed to create whatever they wanted with an assortment of materials. Find out what your child enjoyed at school and incorporate it into your home schooling.

The cons of home educating

Whilst I can fully recommend educating your children at home, I think it's only fair to issue a few warnings about what your journey might entail.

Socialization problems

Although there should not really be any need to worry about socialization problems, this is a subject that needs to be addressed, particularly if you have an only child who is being home educated. When a child is at school they are expected to mix with children of all ages and from all backgrounds. When you take a child out of that system and teach them at home, you will need to ensure that they still socialize with other children, otherwise they can become very withdrawn and isolated and not have any friends to play with.

As discussed in Chapter 08, it's easy to help your child socialize with other children in many different ways, but you do need to be proactive in allowing your children to mix with other people.

Another issue for many young people is the End of Year Prom. Many schools here in the UK have adopted the end of year school celebrations from our American friends; where the girls all dress up in ball gowns and the boys in dinner jackets. A home-educated child can often feel left out from this gathering, especially when he/she still has friends that go to school. An option is to get together with other home educators and throw your own End of Year Party, or encourage your children to have their own party the following week, or take them out for the evening.

Any parent that educates their child at home needs to encourage them to spend as much time as they can with people of their own age, which means organizing regular sleepovers, play dates and being actively involved in their child's free time.

Time management and commitment

If you choose to educate your child at home you need to be prepared to commit your time and energy to it. You can't simply leave a child to get on with reading a book while you pop off to work for a few hours – for one, it's illegal, and two, you are not providing your child with an education by doing that.

Home educating is a huge commitment where at least one parent has to be present at all times. Not only do you have to be prepared to be a parent to your child, but also their teacher and mentor. Home education is a wonderful experience for any family, but your lifestyle will change dramatically when you become one. Your child is no longer out of the house for six hours a day, they are there all the time, and even if they are old enough to get on with work on their own, you still need to be around to answer questions, help with research and guide them. You can't suddenly announce that you're off out for lunch with your friend, unless there is someone to look after the children. As a home educator you have to be prepared to be completely selfless and to put your children's needs before your own. Work has to be fitted in around their learning, which might mean that you have to work evening/night shifts and you have to be able to accept that you will have no time to call your own any more.

Limitations to a parent's career choice

When you are a home educator your working life will change – it has to. You can't continue to work in a 9 a.m. to 5 p.m. office job and educate your children at the same time. Many parents are able to work shifts so that there is always one parent around at any given time. For some, the mum is the main educator whilst the dad continues to work. It isn't as disastrous as you might initially think; I know one family where the mum stays at home with the children during the week days while the dad works a 9–5 office job and then at weekends the mum works as a nurse and the dad looks after the children. Nowdays many companies are also very flexible and some allow working from home or flexi-hours. If you think about it, it is not such a major change to your lifestyle than when children go to school – when they finish school or have half-term breaks, someone still has to be at home to look after them.

Zero funding

As explained earlier in the book, unlike for school-educated children, there is no government funding for children who are educated from home, so everything you buy to meet their educational needs has to come from *your* pocket.

Home educating can cost as much or as little as you wish. If you are teaching in line with the National Curriculum then you will have to pay for the cost of workbooks, material, exams etc. Educational trips out will also have to be paid for by you, but there are many educational places of interest that you can take your children to that are free. The charity Education Otherwise aims to encourage many educational centres to give a discount to home-educated families. Also don't forget about the money you save from not having to pay for school uniforms, lunches and travel, it all helps to compensate.

Private lessons

In many state-funded schools children get extra-curricular lessons, such as drama, music and sport, provided for them for nothing. If you wish your child to learn a musical instrument, as a home-educated child you are not entitled to any funding for these extra lessons. The same goes for sporting activities. If your child shows an interest in a particular sport, you will have to fund that activity yourself. Again, you should ask around at local sports centres and see if they will give you a midweek discount on sporting activities.

Sibling arguments

I was told by my LA Officer to be prepared that our second daughter would soon follow suit and want to be educated at home after we took our eldest daughter out of school, and sure enough she was right. If you have more than one child at home, as with any healthy family there are bound to be arguments and sibling rivalry between them from time to time. This is perfectly normal. Children fight or disagree all the time at school and it's no different at home. Just because they are now being home educated doesn't mean they are going to instantly change their personalities, and just like adults some will be in a mood one day and perfectly fine the next.

My daughters have their fair share of arguments just like any other family and I have learned not to interfere (unless of course blood is drawn!) and let them sort it out for themselves. If you jump in before they have had a chance to debate for themselves they are not learning how to communicate with someone who has a differing opinion. A healthy argument is the sign of a healthy child who knows his/her own mind and is confident enough to feel able to put his/her point across.

Top tip

Don't worry if your children have arguments with each other from time to time, this is perfectly natural.

Inquisitive individuals

I think this is the one thing that I have found most difficult to deal with in all my time as a home educator. I have no problem with LA Officers or officials, but I find it incredibly wearing having to feel as though I have to justify myself to other people who want to quiz me about my choice of education for my children, and this is one of the downsides of being a home educator.

I frequently get annoyed that people I don't even know feel compelled to stop me and question me as to why my children are not in school – What are they doing? Why don't I think the state-education is a fit place for my children to learn when they send their own children there? etc. etc. I don't ask, or have any interest, in where their children go to school, what lessons they are being taught or how many GCSEs they have gained. It doesn't interest me and yet they feel that they have every right to interrogate me.

This is unfortunately something that you will experience when you decide to become a home educator. Friends and even family will question your sanity and you will constantly feel obliged to prove yourself to them and justify your decision that you are only thinking of your child's best interests.

The problem is that although home education is on the increase, the majority of children in this country are still educated at a state-funded school. Anything out of the ordinary is naturally questioned and often misunderstood. As I mentioned in Chapter 04, you can, if you're feeling brave and have the time, point out all that is wrong with our state-educational system and explain your reasons as to why you have chosen to educate your children at home, or you can just ignore them and walk away. I'm afraid that this is one of those occupational hazards that home educators just have to put up with.

LA Officers

As mentioned earlier, if you are going to educate your child at home you are going to come across the LA Officer at some point. Depending on how clued up your LA Officer is about home education will depend on whether this is a pro or a con. LA Officers should be aware of home-educators' rights, but not all are, so it will be up to you to put them in the picture.

Unfortunately dealing with LA Officers is another occupational hazard when you decide to home educate your child. Please do not feel threatened by them. You are aware of your legal rights and you do not have to answer any questions that you feel are inappropriate or have to prove yourself to anyone. I hope that in time all LA Officers will be better informed when dealing with home-educating families and the issues of threats of legal action that have often happened in the past will cease.

Keeping records

As I mentioned in Chapter 07, the need to keep some form of record of your child's education is, although not a legal requirement, advised. This takes up some time, particularly if you have children of different ages and learning levels.

As I mentioned, I try to keep a diary of what we've been working on and keep one page per child; so at the end of the week I jot down what each of them has been doing. I also keep my 'proof' book which is full of photographs of the non-written activities they do such as ice skating. Again, this all takes up time at the end of the week, but if anyone official questions you, you are already prepared with an outline of what the children have learnt and what they have done.

Some home educators do not keep any records of their children's work. This is fine, but personally I think it is important if only to enable your child to see what he/she has achieved. Added to this, if your child wishes to go to college and doesn't have the necessary GCSEs to gain entry, a portfolio of work that he/she has produced will be required.

Different learning levels

It can be a bit of a problem when you have children of differing ages and learning levels to keep up with work for each of them. My children are currently 15, 12 and six so their learning materials are very different from each other, which in turn means that I have to work on different things with each of them.

As a parent you will already know your child's abilities and strengths and what they are capable of learning, so it just means that you will have to spend some time setting work at different levels. I tend to do this on a Sunday evening and ask each one what they would like to work on the following week. There are many free worksheets, resources and games for all ages available on the Internet and some of these are included in Chapter 11.

Children are wonderful at telling you what they want to study and I have found this to be an effective way of setting them work that doesn't feel like work to them. For example, my eldest daughter has studied all the Shakespeare plays after initially watching the modern films based on his plays, such as *She's the Man*. My middle daughter has learned all about primates by the countless visits to our local zoo and my youngest daughter has learnt to read thanks to the Cbeebies website (**www.bbc.co.uk/cbeebies**)!

Research

This isn't a disadvantage as such, in fact much of the time it's great fun. However, it is something that plays a big part in home education and it does involve researching things that you might never have bothered with if you had left your child's learning in the hands of the teachers. Children are naturally inquisitive and want to find out the answers to their many questions all the time. From 'Why is the sky blue?' to 'What speed does a fighter jet fly at?', children want to know the answers and this is when you will find yourself researching subjects you might have no interest in or no inclination to know about!

This all takes up time and you need to be prepared to help your child investigate. Having said this, it is great fun learning about things you never thought of questioning before. For example, one of my children wanted to know how a video recorder worked, so we spent hours dissecting an old video player to discover all about magnetized tape. This is something I wouldn't have had any interest in learning about had it not been for my daughter's inquisitive mind.

Research can be really good fun too. Often we will have a week where we pick a county to study and find out all about the culture, the climate and the cuisine of that country. So, we might decide to study Italy one week and because finances won't stretch to a trip to Venice we will spend the week learning some Italian, cooking traditional Italian foods and learning all about the country from books, CDs and the Internet. Again, this is something that I probably wouldn't research unless I was planning a trip to Italy.

I now know, among other things, how pencils are made, how fast a giraffe can run (35 miles per hour, in case you were wondering), how many siblings Jane Austen had, and how to make an acid/alkaline indicator for cabbages! All things I would never have discovered had my children not demanded to know.

Key points

• As a home educator your family life will change, but for the better.

• People will be naturally curious as to why you wish to educate your children yourself and will want to quiz you about it – this is usually more about them and their choices than you and yours.

finding help

In this chapter you will learn:
- **where to find help**
- **about useful addresses and resources**
- **about qualification information.**

I suppose it is because nearly all children go to school nowadays, and have things arranged for them, that they seem so forlornly unable to produce their own ideas.

Agatha Christie

Help!

We are so used to being told what and how we should teach our children that we tend to forget that children are individuals and are all learning different things at different levels every day of their young lives.

There are very few young people who know what professions they want to join when they are still children. It pays to think back to your own school years. I had dreams of being a vet when I was 14 – until I realized that playing and petting the animals was only a very small part of it! Education should be a fun process and something to look forward to, not something to dread every Sunday evening.

I find it interesting that if you give a child the option of going to school or having the day off to do what they want, the majority of children will opt for the latter. How many times have you heard a celebratory cheer echo around a school playground when the bell rings to signal the end of school and the start of the summer holidays? Or seen the summer holiday adverts declaring, 'School's Out!'? If going to school is so great, why are children glad to see the back of it and why are advertizing companies so happy to celebrate the arrival of the half terms and summer holidays? Talk about mixed messages!

Going to school is portrayed as something children have to put up with, just like we had to. Yes, it's a pain having to get up early and trudge off everyday to sit in a room with 30 other children, but, oh well, we had to do it and so do they. This is the message we send out to our children – a kind of, well, that's-the-way-it-is attitude. I know from my own daughter's experiences of speaking with her school friends, not many have said they would prefer to go to school than stay at home. Does this not say something about our educational system? I don't believe that there is anything that you can learn at school that you can't learn at home if you have the time, resources and dedication.

There are going to be times as a home educator when you will need some help from somewhere and you will spend hours questioning whether or not you are doing the right thing for your children. You will question whether you have the right and the intelligence to call yourself a teacher and wonder how you can possibly teach your children things that you don't know about. There will be times when you feel like banging your head against the wall because you still don't get fractions, and how can you possibly expect your child to get them when you haven't got a clue!

This chapter is designed to put your mind at rest.

Yes, there are going to be times when you feel as though you have made a huge mistake and you cannot possibly know everything there is to know, no one can. But, it pays to remember that you were the person who initially taught your child their basic skills in life: how to walk and talk; how to use a knife and fork; how to dress themselves properly etc. It was your encouragement that helped them in every activity and you are perfectly well equipped to continue to guide them through the rest of their learning.

It doesn't matter if you don't know the process of photosynthesis, you can find out about it with your child and learn as you go along. It doesn't matter that you don't know that the capital of Botswana is Gaborone, or how to say, 'Can I please have an ice cream?' in Arabic. What matters is that you are prepared to give up the time and energy to help your child learn what they want to learn and to give them the encouragement to enjoy learning well beyond their school years.

From a personal point of view I wouldn't change it for the world. I never realized just how much fun it would be to be a home educator. We are also much closer as a family unit and because we see each other every day of the week we have all learned to respect each other, give each other space when we need it and debate in a healthy fashion rather than yell at each other from one side of the room to the other. The subjects that our children have studied are subjects that are of interest to them, rather than being told that they have to study something that they have no interest in. I have also learned a lot more than I would have done had I not given home education a go.

My children have grown into polite and confident young ladies who are not afraid to ask questions or give their opinion. They can hold a healthy debate with people of all ages. Whether or not they would be the same if they attended school is, I guess, open to debate, but somehow I don't think so.

Home-education individuals and organizations

Below is a list of helpful individuals, organizations, informative websites and other guidance available for the home educator.

Deborah Durbin

As the author of this book I thought it only fitting to provide my details should you wish to get in touch with me with any questions, problems or worries about home education. I have educated my children for the past four years and during that time I have learned so much about the educational system and educating from home.

To support this book I have started a website: www.tyhe.webs.com which I try to update as much as possible, or you can reach me through my work website: www.deborah durbin.webs.com

Iris Harrison

Iris Harrison is a campaigner for home educators, having won her own battle against her Local Education Authority in a court case in 1981. One of the original founders of Education Otherwise, Iris now spends her time helping children with dyslexia to benefit from new technology that will help them in reading and writing. Still an advocate for home education, Iris is happy to be contacted by anyone that is having problems with their Local Education Authority.

You can contact Iris by visiting her website at www.speaksvolumes.org.uk

Sally Lever

Sally Lever is, among other things, a home educator and a life coach. In 1998 when she discovered how unhappy her children were at school she started to question the assumptions of compulsory mass schooling and decided to quit her job and educate them from home. She says that the reduction in the family's income meant that they had to readjust their lives and focus their priorities on the family. Sally had to sell her house and she and her husband decided to both work part-time in order to be able to educate their children. Sally is an inspiration to any parent deciding to take on the role of home educator and can help you to adjust your life so that it is more play than work. Sally's website contains pages of articles relating not only to home education but also to downshifting, working from home and readjusting your life so that it is less stressful and more fun.

You can contact Sally by visiting **www.sallylever.co.uk**

Dr Paula Rothermel

Dr Paula Rothermel is an educational psychologist who specializes in home education. It was thanks to Paula and her initial study, which was the first of its kind in the UK, that we have reports on the academic and psychosocial assessments of home-educated children. Her work involves being an expert witness for cases involving home education. Her research has been cited during an adjournment debate in the House of Commons on home education. She is currently based at the University of Durham.

You can contact Dr Rothermel by logging on to her website at **www.paularothermel.co.uk**

Action for Home Education

Action for Home Education, or AHEd for short, is a network of home-educating parents whose experience spans more than 25 years. The group helps both home education groups as well as individuals and is an affiliate of the Scottish home education association, Schoolhouse, who support home-educating families in Scotland. It is also a member of the Centre for Personalized Education Trust, whose trustees include the highly respected, academic researcher of home education, Dr Roland Meighan. The purpose of AHEd is to bring home educators together in a bid to continue the freedom of choice in education for parents and children. It fights for the rights of parents to home educate and in particular for the rights of single parents.

You can contact Action for Home Education by visiting: **www.ahed.org.uk** or by writing to Action for Home Education, PO Box 7324, Derby, DE1 0GT.

Advisory Centre for Education

The Advisory Centre for Education or ACE is a registered national charity that provides independent advice to all parents and carers of children aged between five and 16 in state-funded education. They offer free advice on many subjects from dealing with bullying, school admission appeals and special educational needs, to exclusion from school or advice for anyone that is experiencing problems within the state-school system.

ACE's philosophy is that they believe in a fair education system for everyone and work hard to promote fairness and opportunity for all within education. They have over 45 years combined experience in the field of education and it is an ideal place to go if you or your child has been experiencing problems with a school.

Go to **www.ace-ed.org.uk** to read how ACE might be able to help you.

Education Otherwise

Education Otherwise is a UK charity dedicated to home educators and their families. Originally formed by a small group of parents in 1977, it has grown to become one of the most supportive, self-help organizations in home schooling. The charity offers support, advice and information to families new to home educating as well as to those who have been home educators for a long time. They also have several members that have specialist experience in the legalities of home education.

Education Otherwise or EO as it is often referred to, is by no means anti-school, its aim is to provide parents with the information to choose which is the best form of education for their child/children and believes in informed choice. Its website is a good place to start finding out about home education, your legal rights and any concerns you might have about being a home educator to your children.

Much of the information is available on the website for no fee, but if you become a member (currently £25 per year and £20 for subsequent years) you will be entitled to many extras including a contact list of other home-educating families across the country, a bi-monthly newsletter, a members' handbook, and a family membership card to enable you to ask for discounts on various educational resources.

To contact Education Otherwise, please visit their website at **www.education-otherwise.org** or write to Education Otherwise, PO Box 325, Kings Lynn, PE34 3XW. Helpline 0845 4786345.

A. S. Neill's Summerhill School

A. S. Neill's Summerhill School has been dubbed as the 'world's famous free-school' and was founded in 1921 by Scottish writer and self-proclaimed rebel A. S. Neill as a community in which children could be free from adult authority. The school and his ideas became world famous through Neill's writings and lectures and his books are still published today. Summerhill is the only 'school' that follows the philosophy of home educating that I know of.

Summerhill School is based in Leiston, Suffolk, and is a fee-paying boarding school with a difference. The school does have day pupils but many go on to become boarders by the age of seven. A complete education for Summerhill pupils usually ends at the age of 17 and there are usually between 80 and 90 children, 12 full-time staff and many part-time staff who keep the school running smoothly.

The philosophy behind Summerhill is to allow children to express themselves in a way that is natural to them and focuses on self-esteem and positive personal development. Their holidays are much longer than that of a state-funded school with five weeks at Christmas and spring and nine weeks for the summer.

Pupils are encouraged to take control of their own learning and make their own decisions; this is the only school that I know of its kind that comes anywhere close to home education. Summerhill is nothing like a boarding school in the traditional sense, rather it is somewhere between a tribe and a very large family. It is a very child-centred environment where the adults are friends. All classes at Summerhill are optional and if you want to play all day you can. The subjects your child can study at Summerhill range from academic studies to horse riding and even learning how to be a DJ. Pupils may study for the English GCSE exam if they wish but not all pupils do so and the only homework children get is if they are studying for an exam.

You can find out more about Summerhill School by visiting their website at **www.summerhillschool.co.uk**

Freedom in Education

Freedom in Education was set up by Gareth Lewis as a means of providing information and advice on all aspects of home education. Gareth is the author of two books: *One to One* and *Unqualified Education*, two practical guides for home educators, and is also the editor for the quarterly magazine, *Freedom in Education*. They provide a free e-newsletter and currently have over 1,000 subscribers. The Freedom in Education website contains pages of information for everything from dealing with bullying issues to different learning styles and is a great source of information for everyone involved in home education. There are frequently asked questions, tips on what children want to learn and one of the biggest contact lists for home-educating families.

You can contact Freedom in Education by visiting **www.freedom-in-education.co.uk**

Freedom for Children to Grow

Freedom for Children to Grow is an organisation which fights for parents' rights to educate their children from home. Their website contains details on their latest campaign as well as providing links to useful information.

Visit **www.freedomforchildrentogrow.org** to find out more.

HESFES

The Home Education Seaside Festival, or HESFES as it is more commonly known, is the world's biggest summer festival for home educators. It attracts families from all over the world and is designed as a place where you can take your children for a week-long camping holiday to one of the UK's seaside resorts where there are a host of activities including circus skills, creative writing workshops, drama and dance, crafts, a teen tent, yoga, a bouncy castle, live music and much more.

The HESFES is a chance for parents and children to get together, swap ideas, chat, swim in the sea, and generally enjoy themselves. It is advisable to book early because places get filled very quickly.

For more information please go to **www.hesfes.co.uk**

HE Special UK

HE Special UK is an Internet resource for home-educating families who have children with special needs. Inside their pages you will find information on learning difficulties such as dyslexia, Asperger's syndrome, autism and dyspraxia, in the form of articles and case studies. The website also includes lots of links to other special needs resources.

Please visit **www.he-special.org.uk**

Home Education UK

Home Education UK was set up by Mike Fortune-Wood, a home-educating parent to his four children since 1992. He is also involved in research on behalf of the charity, Personalize Education Now and provides training to Local Authorities on all issues relating to home education. Mike does not charge for any information or assistance to parents wishing to home educate, rather he relies on donations to help him keep the website up and running.

The Home Education website is full of all the information a home-educating parent will ever need and Mike is on hand to answer any questions that might arise as you start out on your home-educating journey.

You can order a copy of Mike's journal, *The Home Education Journal*, which is published three times a year, through the website. The journal will keep you up to date with news, events, changes in legislation and much more.

Visit **www.home-education.org.uk** for more information.

Interhigh

Interhigh is one of the many Internet schools that have popped up in recent years. It is modelled on the modern UK/Welsh secondary school and is suitable for children aged between seven and 16. Teachers and pupils work from home by logging into a virtual classroom on the Internet to receive real-time tuition every weekday morning. Apart from lessons, teachers set and mark homework, give reports, set end of year exams and prepare pupils for the GCSEs and A Levels of their choice.

Admission to Interhigh is limited to just 30 students in each school year. It is therefore necessary to apply as soon as possible to ensure your place is reserved; the school can take applications throughout the year. After the initial registration you will receive a Conditions of Attendance form to be completed.

At the time of writing, a place at Interhigh will cost you £2,100 for a year and fees can be paid in instalments. If you wish your children to continue to follow the National Curriculum but also be home educated, this is an ideal option as they will receive all the lessons required for GCSE exams. Obviously, you will need a computer and a reliable Internet connection for Internet-based learning, but it is an ideal option for children who want to learn at home but who also want a more structured way of learning.

You can find out more by visiting **www.interhigh.co.uk**

Kidscape

Set up in 1984 by psychologist Dr Michele Elliott, Kidscape was the first charity in the UK to focus specifically on the prevention of bullying and child sexual abuse. With the help of parents, carers, teachers, police and other caring professionals, children are taught ways to deal with bullies, good self-defence and how to deal with approaches from strangers.

Where other charities offer after-the-event support, Kidscape works to keep children safe before harm occurs. Kidscape's work is based on the premise that:

- all children have the right as individuals to the knowledge and skills that will help them to be safe, independent and able to express their feelings and concerns; and
- all adults have the responsibility to keep children safe, to listen to their feelings and concerns and take them seriously.

Kidscape was the first nationwide prevention programme for children dealing with personal safety. Kidcape's child protection programmes are based on three pilot projects. The first project (1984–6) involved a two-year study with 4,000 children, parents and teachers. Although 'stranger danger' was widely taught to children by police school liaison officers, the pilot studies revealed that the main threat to children was in fact from people known to them – bullies, friends, or even family members.

Kidscape programmes are now taught UK-wide in thousands of schools and community groups. Over 2 million children throughout the UK have been taught Kidscape's Child Protection Programme, although this figure grows every day. Every year they advise over 12,000 children and parents through their anti-bullying helpline and distribute over 250 bully-packs each week.

If your child has suffered at the hands of a bully, contact Kidscape in confidence by visiting **www.kidscape.org.uk** or phone their helpline on 08451 205 204.

Montessori Teaching

Montessori Schools UK is an informative website for anyone interested in the Montessori method of teaching (see Chapter 06). It lists schools, books, educational resources and training materials for anyone interested in teaching the Montessori method and also outlines the philosophy behind Maria Montessori's teachings. There is also a members' area that you can join along with a members' forum, so plenty of online help is available if you need it.

To find out more about the Montessori method visit **www.montessori.org.uk**

Muddle Puddle

Muddle Puddle is a home-educating website that is intended for home-educating families with children aged up to eight years old. The site offers advice for parents of younger children, with tips and ideas for 'lessons' such as teaching your child to read and learning maths in an un-boring way.

Muddle Puddle also organizes a summer camp where other families can meet up, swap tips and ideas and generally have a nice time together. The site also contains many different learning style ideas such as Montessori and educational philosophies.

Log on to **www.muddlepuddle.co.uk** for further information.

Schoolhouse

The Schoolhouse Home Education Association was founded in 1996 by a group of home-educating families who wished to raise public awareness of the issues surrounding home education in Scotland.

Schoolhouse is a recognized charity and offers information and support to those who wish to take personal responsibility for the education of their children. Schoolhouse members share skills, resources, information and ideas with each other and often hold get-togethers and events for their members, from major conferences and seminars to informal meetings and family days out. Schoolhouse regularly participates in consultations with the Scottish Executive, local authorities and voluntary groups and is regularly invited to attend teacher-training programmes.

Schoolhouse also has established links with other UK home-educating organizations that promote educational freedom, including Personalized Education Now, Home Education UK and Action on Rights for Children. They also have contacts with home-educating networks across Europe, the USA, Australia and Japan.

As a charity they survive solely on subscriptions and donations. You can contact Schoolhouse by visiting their website at **www.schoolhouse.org.uk**

Steiner Education

The Steiner method of education is based on the understanding of the child as a whole and works for all children regardless of their age and abilities. Based on the work of Dr Rudolf Steiner (1861–1925), a philosopher and scientist who inspired what has become a worldwide movement of schools that promote universal human values, educational and meaningful teaching and learning opportunities. This progressive, international school's movement is noted by educationalists, doctors, policy makers and parents for the effective education that it offers children. Formal learning of the three Rs does not feature in the Steiner education curriculum, instead the belief is that a child will learn these skills more effectively if he/she has had plenty of time and opportunity to first develop socially, emotionally and physically in a creative, secure and harmonious environment.

Many home educators follow the Steiner philosophy and you can find out more about it by visiting **www.steinerwaldorf.org**

The British Dyslexia Association

The British Dyslexia Association is a dyslexia friendly group that helps all dyslexic people regardless of age or ability. The association promotes early identification and supports all sufferers in a bid to help them attain their goals. They also help dyslexic learners that are of a school-leaving age and who are either going to college or looking for employment.

The site also has an online shop that sells equipment to enable dyslexic suffers to learn more easily, including accessible and enjoyable fiction books for children and young adults and a reading tool that will read back any text displayed on a computer screen as it is typed.

Dyslexia is a complex condition which affects each person differently, and the severity can vary from person to person. The BDA is able to help anyone that suffers from dyslexia, mild or severe.

Contact them by visiting **www.bdadyslexia.org.uk** or phoning 0845 251 9002.

Internet educational resources

Below are some of the best educational resources that I have used in my journey of home education.

ABC Teach

Although an American site, ABC Teach is another free Internet resource where you can download hundreds of worksheets designed for younger children. The site contains information and worksheets ranging from studying the seasons to practising handwriting and using printable word flashcards.

Visit **www.abcteach.com** for further information.

BBC History

The BBC history website is a great resource for anyone who is interested in history. It is simple to use and contains a timeline to show various historical events. The site includes a daily 'on this day in history' and a selection of links to fun and educational activities such as History for kids, Family history where you can research your family tree and History trails which helps you use source material to uncover history. Great fun for budding historians.

Visit **www.bbc.co.uk/history**

Cbeebies

The BBC's Cbeebies website is an excellent source of information for children under the age of seven. The site is packed with things to do: colouring pages, quizzes, games, music and ideas for things to make and do. This site encourages children to use many skills via the computer.

Visit **www.bbc.co.uk/cbeebies**

Cool Math 4 Kids

This site not only makes maths fun but it also explains in an easy way how maths works. The site has brainteasers, maths jigsaw puzzles and lots of other fun games. Never before was maths so cool!

Children will have hours of fun on the Cool Math 4 Kids website **www.coolmath4kids.com**

Direct Gov

Direct Gov is the official government website for information relating to everything from the National Curriculum to employment laws. The site covers everything you will need to know about the National Curriculum, including all the Key Stages, and any new updates to educational testing, exams and new introductions such as the New Diploma and the Modern Apprenticeships.

You can keep up to date with educational changes by visiting **www.direct.gov.uk**

Ed Place Science

Ed Place Science is a great resource for any parent who doesn't know much about the subject but wants their child to learn it. It is a unique online source of everything scientific and has lots of wonderful worksheets designed for Key Stages 1–4. At the time of writing the cost of using Ed Place starts at £9.99 per month for one subject, £16.98 for two subjects and £21.98 for three subjects. It covers science, maths and English and has an 'Ask the Teacher' section where you can email a teacher a question and receive a reply within 24 hours.

For more information visit **www.edplace.co.uk**

Home Education in the UK

Home Education in the UK is a resourceful website with pages of information for the new home educator and covers everything from what home educating is about to de-registering your child from school, a typical home-education day, socialization issues, and educational resources, to name but a few. The site is an honest look at what it's really like to home educate your child and what you will probably encounter along the way.

For more information visit **http://home-ed.info**

National Extension College

With over 150 home-study courses and 200 resource titles, the National Extension College has something to offer everyone. They have been providing distance learning courses for over 40 years and they welcome home-educated children on all of their courses and offer good discounts. Courses range from the standard GCSEs to certificates in arts, health and fitness.

For more information contact **www.nec.ac.uk** or telephone 0800 389 2839.

Oxford Home Schooling

Oxford Home Schooling has been in the business of education for 18 years and provides learning materials specifically for home-educated children. All courses are written and tutored by experts and provide a comprehensive coverage of the syllabus. They also offer easy payment plans for each of their courses.

For more information visit **www.oxfordhomeschooling. co.uk**

Parents in Touch

You can often feel isolated when you become a home-educating parent because the majority of parents still send their children to a state-funded school, so you often feel like the only person on the planet with different views. This is where Parents in Touch comes to the rescue. Along with pages of information relating to home education, the website also offers a parents' forum where you can discuss issues relating to home education, swap ideas and tips and generally feel as though you have like-minded people to talk to when you need it. The site also offers a wealth of information about home educating and has over 4,000 worksheets available to members.

For more information visit **www.parentsintouch.co.uk**

Primary Home Education UK

Primary Home Education UK is an Internet resource specifically designed for parents who are planning to educate their primary-aged children from home, whether they live in the UK or overseas. Their curriculum packs are written by qualified primary teachers for home-educating families rather than for primary teachers in school settings. The materials in a Primary Home Education UK pack gives comprehensive daily and weekly teaching plans for English, maths and science and shows you how to teach each topic to your child. The packs include worksheets, activity sheets and games to practise the skills they have learned in each lesson; they also include a variety of teaching strategies to use for key points, so you can tailor the teaching method to the way your child learns best.

The packs follow the National Curriculum in England and Wales and are updated to include the latest national numeracy and literacy stages. There is tutor support included, so if you have any problems you or your child has someone to ask.

At the time of writing, the cost of a curriculum pack starts at £510 per term for Years 1–6 or £128 per month. Reception material starts at £209 per term or £53 per month.

For more information visit **www.primaryhomeeducation.co.uk**

School History

For history buffs who want to learn what children at school are learning, this is an ideal resource. You can plan lessons in accordance with your child's age or you can choose a single subject to study if you wish. School History has over 650 free downloads and over 80 PowerPoint presentations. There are lots of interactive games, quizzes and GCSE online revision programmes to use.

Visit **www.schoolhistory.co.uk** for further information.

Superkids

Superkids is a great Internet resource where you can make and then print off your own free maths worksheets and answer sheets for your children. The site allows you to set as many calculations as you would like per page and covers everything from basic addition and subtraction to fractions and percentages.

You can find out more by visiting **www.superkids.com**

The Freecycle Network

The Freecycle Network is, as the name suggests, a recycling website where you can recycle anything from books to furniture for free. Rather than throw good stuff away you can log on to the Freecycle Network and offer it to a good home for nothing and at the same time you can get things that you need for free. Depending on what area you live in there are hundreds of items for free listed on the site and your only expense will be to collect the items you are interested in. A quick look at the educational section whilst writing this book brought up a set of GCSE revision books, a globe of the world, a full stamp collection, a sports bike and a set of animal encyclopaedias.

Visit **www.freecycle.org**

The Loch Ness Project

The Loch Ness Project is a wonderful resource for anyone who wants to study all about the legendary Scottish monster. There is a special section for young Nessy enthusiasts where you can download free activity sheets, jigsaws and a place where your child can add their own ideas about what Nessy really is. There are a number of interesting articles on The Loch Ness Project which is a fascinating resource for children and adults alike.

Visit **www.lochnessproject.org** for further information.

The Mind Kind Way

The Mind Kind Way is a good resource for all home educators who want software or educational resources. The Mind Kind Way website has many free downloads so you can try before you buy and the materials cover Key Stages 3, 4 and above.

For further information visit **www.mindkindway.com**

Tutorvista

Tutorvista is an Internet website that will help your child build a strong foundation for future study. The site has dedicated tutors for all subjects from Key Stage 1 to AS and A Levels. Similar to the Interhigh school, Tutorvista learning is learning from the comfort of your own home and is also affordable. They can sort out GCSE and A Level exams for you so that you don't have the hassle of finding an exam centre.

Visit **www.tutorvista.co.uk** for more information.

Helpful books

Deceptive Encounters by Karen J. Jones

Deceptive Encounters is a fictional book written by scientist and author, Karen J. Jones. The book supports the National Curriculum for science and is particularly suitable for Key Stage 2 and 3 pupils. The story is about two schoolgirls, Emma Waldron and Lauren Bale, who find themselves implicated in a manslaughter and missing person investigation when their plans for a clandestine overnight beach party with friend, Jamie Jackson, take an unexpected turn.

An injury sustained whilst rock climbing, during an afternoon truanting, forces the two young girls to shelter overnight in a cave at the tiny seaside resort of Longbarrow. It is here that they stumble upon their fugitive teacher, Luke Michael, who is in hiding, following a recent hit-and-run incident. A series of chance discoveries leads Detective Constable Steve Turnbull, and Crime Scene Investigator, Alexia Stermont, to join forces and embark on the trail of forensic evidence, ranging from fingerprinting and toxicology to DNA profiling, in an aim to solve the case of missing teenager, Angela Stoker.

Karen's book is suitable for children from ten upwards and provides a wealth of information on the subject of science and forensics. The book is available by visiting **www.troubador.co.uk/book_info.asp?bookid=713**

Free-Range Education – How Home Education Works by Terri Dowty

Free-Range Education is a handbook for families considering or starting out in home education. The book, written in 2003, is packed with resources, stories, questions and practical tips to advise the new home educator. It includes legalities and is written in a no-nonsense style. The book, published by Hawthorn Press, is available to buy from **www.amazon.co.uk**

How Children Fail by John Holt

First published in the mid 1960s, *How Children Fail* began an education reform movement that continues today. In his 1982 edition, John Holt added new insights into how children investigate the world, the perennial problems of classroom learning, grading, testing, and the role of trust and authority in every learning situation. His understanding and deep affection for children and the clarity of his thought have made both *How Children Fail* and its companion volume, *How Children Learn*, enduring classics. Both are available from **www.amazon.co.uk**

How Children Learn at Home by Alan Thomas and Harriet Pattison

How Children Learn at Home is the book compiled from Alan Thomas and Harriet Pattison's academic study into home-educated children and is an excellent source of information Their investigation provides not only an insight into the powerful and effective nature of informal learning but also presents some fundamental challenges to many of the assumptions underpinning educational theory. This book will be of interest to education practitioners, researchers and all parents, whether their children are in or out of school, offering fascinating insights into the nature of children's learning. You can find *How Children Learn at Home* by visiting **www.amazon.co.uk**

The Unschooling Handbook by Mary Griffith

The Unschooling Handbook by Mary Griffith is primarily aimed at the American market but it contains a lot of information on learning styles and reassures the reader that children have a fantastic ability to teach themselves and that they do not necessarily learn just by sitting at a desk and reading from a book. Mary has included a number of case studies within the book which give the reader first-hand experiences of what home education is really like. *The Unschooling Handbook* is available from **www.amazon.co.uk**

helping your child to read
dee reid & diana bentley

- Do you want your child to become a confident reader?
- Do you need advice on how to develop your child's reading?
- Would you like to support your child's reading at school?

Helping Your Child to Read shows you how to develop your child's reading skills and foster a love of books from birth to the end of their primary school years. It is full of practical advice that will help your child to become a fluent and proficient reader.

Dee Reid and **Diana Bentley** are independent language consultants and Fellows of Oxford Brookes University. They are literacy experts and between them have written over 100 books helping children to read.

teach
yourself

helping your child to get fit
ceri roberts

- Are you worried your child doesn't get enough exercise?
- Do you want to help them find physical activities they enjoy?
- Do you need to improve your child's eating habits?

Helping Your Child to Get Fit will give you practical advice on how to boost your child's activity levels and get them interested in sports and physical activities. It shows you how to make exercise fun and interesting for your child, and gives you lots of suggestions for things to do as a family, as well as nutritional advice and help if you're concerned about your child's weight.

Ceri Roberts is a freelance journalist who specializes in parenting, health and well-being, and who writes regularly for *Practical Parenting* magazine.

teach
yourself

bringing up happy children
glenda weil and doro marden

- Do you want to be a confident parent?
- Do you need help to resolve family disputes?
- Do you want a secure and happy child?

Bringing Up Happy Children will help you to enjoy a happy
and harmonious home, offering supportive advice and practical
strategies. From understanding your parenting style to tackling
difficult issues, it gives everything you need to establish a warm
environment in which your child can flourish.

Glenda Weil and **Doro Marden** have many years' experience
running parenting education groups. Both work with Parentline
Plus, the UK's leading parenting charity. They have seven
children between them.

teach
yourself

things to do as a family
debbie musselwhite

- Would you like to enjoy cheap, fun days out together?
- Do you need boredom-busting tips for long car journeys?
- Would you like great ideas for rainy days and holidays?

Things to do as a Family will give you hundreds of activities that your children can enjoy. With everything from tips on making great fancy dress costumes to practical suggestions for long summer holidays and cheap family days out, it is full of games, hobbies and activities for any age, budget or occasion.

Debbie Musselwhite is a freelance writer who has written widely on parenting and childcare.

teach yourself	**parenting your teenager** suzie hayman

- Do you want better communication between you and your child?
- Do you need help tackling the difficult issues?
- Would you like to help them become confidently independent?

Parenting Your Teenager shows you how to improve communication with your teenager, gives you better insight into your and their behaviour, and helps you tackle conflict calmly. You will become a confident, competent parent, helping your child become a strong, independent young adult.

Suzie Hayman is a Relate-trained counsellor known for her television and media work, a trustee of Parentline Plus, and the author of over 25 books, including **Teach Yourself Successful Step-Parenting** and **Teach Yourself Single Parenting**.

teach yourself

good study skills
bernice walmsley

- Are you a new or out-of-practice learner?
- Do you want tips for reading, reviewing – and passing?
- Do you need help writing projects?

Whether you have just started an evening or training course or even driving lessons, **Good Study Skills** will help you study effectively. From speed reading to writing essays and presentations, it is full of practical techniques, step-by-step instructions and review tests to practice your new skills. With help for those baffled by technology and ample supporting resources, it is ideal for any new or returning learner.

Bernice Walmsley is a full-time writer specializing in educational and business learning.